Living Through History

THE GREAT DEPRESSION

NATHANIEL HARRIS

B.T. Batsford Ltd London

CONTENTS

© Nathaniel Harris 1988
First published 1988

Typeset by Tek-Art Ltd, West Wickham, Kent
and printed and bound by
Richard Clay Ltd,
Chichester, Sussex
for the publishers
B.T. Batsford Ltd
4 Fitzhardinge Street
London W1H 0AH

ISBN 0 7134 5658 2

Cover Illustrations
The colour painting is "Disaster on Wall Street,
1929" (*Giancarlo Costa, Milan*); the portrait is of
Ellen Wilkinson by George Patterson (*Bede
Gallery, Jarrow*); the black and white photograph
shows a slum in Britain in the 1930s (*BBC Hulton
Picture Library*).

THE DEPRESSION YEARS

As experienced by its victims, the Great Depression can be summarized in a phrase: it was the hardest of hard times. For at least a decade – from 1930 until about 1940 – unemployment, poverty, hunger and homelessness blighted millions of lives in the world's richest and most industrially advanced societies. Of course, there had been hard times before, and underprivileged and poverty-stricken groups existed in even the most prosperous of countries. But by the 1920s it was generally assumed – especially in the United States – that production would keep on rising despite occasional setbacks, making most of the population better off from one year to the next. Instead, a financial collapse in 1929 was followed by a general economic decline that continued for years with only intermittent signs of improvement. Production fell dramatically, factories closed, banks failed, and the queues at labour exchanges, dole offices and soup-kitchens grew even longer. This was the Great Depression, which scarred the memories of an entire generation; for many it was a deeper, more bitter experience even than the Second World War, which followed and "cured" it.

The financial collapse that triggered the Depression occurred on the New York Stock Exchange, which is often called "Wall Street" after the thoroughfare on which it stands. A stock exchange is essentially a marketplace in which stocks and shares are bought and sold. Stocks and shares are issued by a business or industrial company, which sells them in order to finance its operations. The most common type of stock literally consists of shares *in* the company: that is, the buyer becomes the owner of a part of the company. The average shareholder owns no more than a fraction of one per cent of the company (or companies) he or she has invested in, and large companies have thousands of shareholders. In the normal course of events, the shareholder expects to

1 The Great Depression was triggered by "the Crash" – the collapse of share values on the New York Stock Exchange. This newspaper headline of 25 October 1929 conveys something of its dramatic impact.

2 Panic and dismay on Wall Street, outside the New York Stock Exchange, where mounted police keep the crowd moving on.

receive a more or less regular dividend – a sum of money which represents his or her share of the company's profits.

In theory, therefore, the prices at which shares change hands will be determined by the value of the company's assets and/or the profits it is expected to make. However, these are not so easily discovered, and many other factors influence share prices, including a general optimism (or pessimism) about the state of the economy as a whole. When business in general is doing well profits are likely to rise and buying shares becomes an attractive prospect. As in most economic transactions, increased demand (more people wanting to buy) tends to push up the price; and if share prices keep rising, more and more people are likely to buy, hoping to sell again later at a still higher price. They are not investors, buying because they believe the company will do well, but *speculators*, buying because they believe the company's share values will increase. The distinction between investment and speculation, though rarely clear cut, is a valuable one. The speculator is "playing the market". He (or she) is a mercurial character, equally prone to enthuse or to panic, and his (her) activities have often made stock markets dangerously unstable institutions.

During the 1920s, speculation ran riot on Wall Street. The United States had emerged unscathed from the First World War of 1914-18, which had greatly weakened the major European economies; both winners and losers ended by owing money to the Americans. Subsequently, American production and productivity soared, the country exported more than it imported, and confidence in "the American way" was never higher. In this boom atmosphere, share prices were driven higher and higher. It seemed that all you needed to do in order to make money was to buy shares, even if you had to borrow heavily to begin with. Stock Exchange regulations made it easy to obtain credit, since investors could buy "on margin", putting down only a percentage of the purchase price. The dangers of this practice seemed purely theoretical: in reality, the more you succeeded in borrowing,

the more money you were likely to make. The New York *Times* industrial average (a day-by-day average figure calculated from the prices of a group of important industrial shares) gives some idea of the way in which the market moved upwards. At the end of May 1924 the average stood at 106; seven months later it was 134; by the end of 1927 it had reached 245. 1928 was an amazing year in which the average rose by 86 points to reach 331; yet it hardly compared with 1929, when a burst of summer madness pushed the figure over 450 by the beginning of September. Share values now bore no relation to the assets or prospects of the companies concerned, and a very large number of companies had been created to meet the insatiable demand for new shares. Most of the new organizations had no function other than to control other companies or deal in their shares; in other words, insubstantial paper empires proliferated.

The bubble had to burst; but the process was not as swift and simple as this image suggests. From 3 September 1929 the market began to slide downwards, but with intermittent rallies that encouraged false hopes. Many shareholders, believing that the market had hit rock bottom at last, held on, or even went back into the market, until further losses turned what might have been a misfortune into a disaster. Borrowers found themselves in terrible straits, and more and more people who had bought on margin found themselves unable to bridge the gap between their debts and the new, low value of their holdings. As these were sold off, panic increased and prices fell still further. Just as prices had once been pushed up by increasing demand (the activities of seemingly insatiable buyers), so now they were depressed by the huge volume of supply – sellers, desperate to unload, who were joined by new masses of sellers as prices continued to slide. On "Black Thursday", 24 October, 16 million shares changed hands and total collapse seemed imminent. Then the nation's leading

3 Those who bought and sold shares – people like ▶ this rueful stockholder – were the first sufferers during the Crash. But millions of ordinary people were soon affected by the Depression that followed.

4

financiers stepped in to buy huge numbers of shares and restore confidence. But the respite was short-lived. The following week the selling started again, and prices went down and down with only occasional breaks. The swarming, ticker-tape-strewn scenes on the floor of the stock exchange, captured for us on newsreel, convey mass panic and hysteria better than most equivalent records of wartime terror. The Great Crash ended at last on 13 November 1929, when the New York *Times* industrials stood at 224, almost 230 points down from their early September peak.

The Crash had ended, but the Depression had hardly begun. Though painful, the Crash itself affected only a minority of Americans; the total number of stock exchange investors and speculators was only about one and a half million, not all of whom made heavy losses. But, as the historian of the Crash, J.K. Galbraith, notes:

To millions of workers, farmers, sharecroppers, and small merchants the devastation of those October days was more distant news. They could not suppose that they were much affected by what was going on in Wall Street. They were very, very wrong. Within months, and for many within weeks, the events in downtown New York had extended their effect to eliminate jobs, reduce prices, close banks, foreclose mortgages. (*The Great Crash*)

Financial panics usually have disruptive effects on national economies, but the impact of the Crash was exceptionally severe. As David Landes explains in his book *The Unbound Prometheus*,

In a highly integrated economy, this kind of collapse builds up in mass and momentum like an avalanche or a landslide. Each man calls upon his debtors for help in meeting the claims of his creditors, so that even the healthiest enterprises are hard pressed to meet the demands that crowd in upon them . . . . The weaker firms, the swollen industrial empires with watered stock and large debts went first; but they dragged some of the strongest companies down with them.

The consequent collapse of confidence also led to massive withdrawals of bank deposits, often fed by wild rumours about the impending failure of given banks. But since a bank operates by using the money deposited with it – not by holding it all immediately available – a sustained "run on the bank" may well bring it into difficulties. In the aftermath of the Crash, people's fears of bank failures led to such sustained "runs", which had the effect of making the rumours come true. Bank after bank was unable to meet the claims made on it and was forced to close. Within a few years of the Crash no less than 5000 American banks failed, with calamitous results. The calling in of loans by stricken banks and frightened investors hit debtors of all kinds – people buying their homes through mortgages, farmers trying to weather times that were hard even before the Depression, and businessmen who hoped to get started, to expand, or just to survive. Through bankruptcies and fore-closures, and in many other ways, the Great Crash soon affected millions who knew nothing of the working of stock exchanges.

For most ordinary people, the worst result of all was mass unemployment. The closing down of factories and banks threw both blue-collar (manual) and white-collar workers into the dole queue. Since the unemployed workers and their families could not afford to buy as much as they had done before, there was less demand for many goods and services. Therefore factories were required to produce less, and needed fewer workers; and so they laid off some of their employees, whose loss of purchasing power reduced demand still further and made even more jobs superfluous – a knock-on effect, or vicious descending spiral, that seemed never-ending.

For this was not like many earlier crises, which spread gloom and ruin but nevertheless wore themselves out after a few months. The Depression went on month after month and year after year, despite regular predictions by the American president, Herbert Hoover, that prosperity was "just around the corner". On the stock exchange, prices continued to fall steadily, so that by July 1932 the *Times* industrials stood at 58 points, indicating that stocks were now worth about one-eighth of their value at the beginning of September 1929. Banks continued to fail and factories to close. Industrial production slumped (by 1933 the Gross National Product of the United States was only one third of the 1929 figure), and unemployment rose until there were almost 13 million Americans without work.

There is no simple, certain explanation for the long duration of the Great Depression, although economists have identified various weaknesses in the organization of American business and industry. Another factor was certainly the unstable state of the international economy, which made it inevitable that in the early 1930s the Depression would spread beyond the USA and have a disastrous effect on world trade.

Europe had made a good deal of economic progress during the 1920s, although her prosperity was a patchier and more fragile matter than that of the American "New Era". Europe had been shattered by the First World War, and her precarious recovery was built largely on American loans. These made it possible for Germany and Austria to pay reparations (compensation, extorted because of their supposed "war guilt") to France and

4 Conditions in British slum areas were quite bad enough even before "the Slump", as the Depression was often called in Britain. ▶

Britain, who were in turn enabled to keep up payments on the debts they had contracted during the war – debts owed mainly to the United States. America was, therefore, caught up in a circular process, making loans to pay off or service earlier American loans. Here was another house of cards, waiting to be flung down by an adverse wind. In the wake of the Crash, when Americans stopped lending and short-term loans began to be called in, the European economy quickly showed signs of strain, and unemployment rose sharply. Then, in May 1931, one of the great European banks, the Kreditanstalt of Vienna, failed. Austrian prosperity collapsed. Foreign investors withdrew their funds from central Europe, bankruptcies and unemployment mounted rapidly in Germany, and within a few weeks Britain too was overtaken by the crisis. France, less industrialized and self-sufficient in agriculture, was not severely affected at first, but by 1931 her economy was

also suffering. The Depression even reached out beyond Europe and North America, since falling demand meant a collapse in the prices of foodstuffs and raw materials. This hit primary producers such as the Brazilian coffee-grower, the Australian sheep-farmer and the Indonesian sugar-grower.

One important way in which governments reacted to the crisis was to impose tariffs on imports from other countries. These heavy duties placed on foreign goods were intended to make them more expensive in the shops, so that people would prefer home-produced goods, on which the manufacturers had not had to pay tariffs. A country's hard-hit industries would therefore be able to carry on, knowing that they could at least find buyers in the home market. This policy – Protectionism – was an understandable response to the Depression, but by drastically reducing the volume of world trade it delayed the longed-for general recovery.

Tariffs apart, countries tackled the Depression in widely different ways. In the United States, a new president, Franklin D. Roosevelt, introduced the "New Deal", which involved using the power of the federal government to help industry and provide jobs. The British reaction was in a more orthodox private enterprise tradition: the government would balance its budget, believing that a sound financial position would eventually lead to recovery – though in the meantime this meant slashing government spending by paying public servants less and reducing the dole money issued to the unemployed. In Germany, where the disruption was greatest, the racist, militaristic, anti-democratic Nazi Party took power under its Führer (Leader), Adolf Hitler. Despite the repugnance often expressed for its political outlook, the new Germany impressed many observers by its economic success, notably in reducing unemployment figures. Intentionally or otherwise, the Nazis embraced the theory associated with the economist John Maynard Keynes, who favoured massive state expenditure on public works to create jobs and get the economic system going again. Unfortunately, Hitler's "public works" consisted of rearmament with a view to

5 In Germany, the Depression undermined the recently established democratic republic. The Nazi Party, led by Adolf Hitler, took over the state.

German expansion, and the building of a huge motorway (*Autobahn*) system whose peacetime usefulness was less important in his mind than its contribution to swift military movement! But despite its ominous content, the Nazi policy seemed to bring economic results.

The rise of Nazism was symptomatic of a widespread disillusionment with established values. Political democracy, unchecked free enterprise, and free trade between nations could no longer command the unquestioning support of the suffering millions. Although many people were willing to believe that the Depression was a kind of unavoidable natural catastrophe, others blamed the political and economic system and strove to change it. Their point of view seemed all the more plausible because the Depression created "poverty amid plenty". It was *not* a collapse of productive capacity, which might have been put down to shortage of resources; for although production did decline sharply, factories and warehouses actually remained overstocked with goods that people could not afford to buy. Mass-production promised abundance for all; yet "the system" kept the goods and their only possible consumers apart. The situation was even more ludicrous where agricultural produce was concerned. Farmers suffered because prices were so low; yet hungry people could still not afford foodstuffs, and had to look on while quantities were simply destroyed. At a time when such things could happen, the capitalist system could be perceived as not merely chaotic and incompetent, but fundamentally inhumane.

One alternative that seemed to provide an escape from this madness was socialism, which promised a society based on common ownership of resources and fair shares for all. Some socialist parties – the British Labour Party, for example, and the German Social Democrats – were committed to using democratic parliamentary means. Others, notably the Communist Parties which had sprung up in many countries, argued that change would have to be brought about by revolution. They pointed out that their brand of socialism was already established in one country, the Soviet Union (USSR), which was being rapidly transformed into an industrial giant through a series of Five Year Plans. In the uncertain atmosphere of the 1930s, the idea of a planned economy held a strong appeal; and the fact that the USSR remained practically untouched by the Depression seemed to demonstrate the superiority of the socialist system. Sections of the French and German working classes were won over to communism, but in Britain and the United States it influenced only a minority of militants, writers and intellectuals, especially among the young. Yet although their numbers were small, these men and women of the Left had a disproportionally strong impact upon the consciousness of their time.

Fascism also had a wide appeal. It was not new: the first Fascist Party had been founded in Italy, where its leader ("Il Duce"), Benito Mussolini, had taken power in 1920. Mussolini had been able to exploit the economic discontents and class antagonisms of Italian society, and the distresses of the 1930s provided new opportunities for fascists of other countries. Fascists despised democracy and made a cult of leadership and obedience; they glorified war; they operated through uniformed military-style organizations which substituted street-fighting for argument; and when they took power they created militarized, hierarchical societies in which no political opposition was permitted. During the 1930s the most spectacular fascist success was the Nazi seizure of power in Germany, which was a direct result of the Depression; the Nazi brand of fascism had an especially poisonous feature in its conviction that the Germans were a "master race" destined to wipe out the Jews, enslave the Slavs, and become lords of vast areas of Europe. Fascism played upon national pride and suspicion of foreigners, promised "order" in place of economic and social chaos, and provided jobless and disoriented people with fixed positions in the black- or brown-shirted fascist private armies. It also offered such people the illusion of decisive action, if only in the opportunity to work off their resentments on political enemies. Mussolini and Hitler had many imitators, successful and otherwise, and in several other countries – for example, Austria, Poland and Greece – democracy was overthrown and authoritarian (if not precisely fascist) governments were established. In the late 1930s fascism continued to advance, despite attempts by liberals, socialists and communists to oppose it with "Popular Front" movements. German and Italian aggressions succeeded again and again. The fascist General Franco overthrew the Spanish Republic with help from Hitler and Mussolini. And in the Far East, a Depression-hit Japan also swung on to a nakedly militaristic course. Understandably, there were observers who believed that the "age of democracy" was coming to an end.

These political facts were part of the texture of the Depression, which can hardly be understood in isolation. All the same, it must be remembered that millions of people continued to vote for conservative or middle-of-the-road political parties. In the dramatic protests made by the victims of the Depression – for example, in Britain, the

Jarrow March – most of those who took part were not revolutionaries, but just people who wanted more help – or simple justice – from the existing system. And even these were a minority. Most of the victims were too confused – perhaps even too physically weakened – to do more than endure until the hard times finally ended.

In the late 1930s there were some hopeful signs. Production picked up and the number of unemployed diminished, although the total figure remained horrifyingly large. The overall situation became less easy to characterize; in Britain, for example, the 1930s were good times for many people, especially in the south of England. But the "black spots" remained, and there were occasional alarms and crises to keep old fears alive. The Depression lingered on into the

6 Millions of people were set on the move during the Depression, driven from their homes or desperate to find work. Both reasons motivated these refugees from the worked-out "dust bowl" of Oklahoma, who drove thousands of miles in their ancient automobiles, hoping to start a new life.

next decade. Then, ironically, the political tensions which had so largely been created by the Depression came to a climax that snuffed it out. A European war between the democracies and the fascist powers broke out in 1939. In 1941 the Soviet Union, Japan and the United States were drawn in, making the conflict world-wide. Now production soared under governments determined to overcome all obstacles; and now there were jobs for all in the armed forces, in the factories or on the land. The Great Depression was over at last.

VICTIMS

Studs Terkel (1912-   )

Louis "Studs" Terkel grew up and completed his studies in Chicago during the early years of the Depression. As he recounts in his autobiographical memoir, *Talking to Myself*, he then discovered that

In the late thirties, as the streets were walked by more than streetwalkers, my diploma from the University of Chicago Law School was of some value, I'm certain. No one told me precisely what.

Like many others during the Depression, Terkel earned a few dollars in any way he could. Having an engagingly villainous-looking face, he posed for a photographer and appeared as a gangster in a detective magazine. He wangled occasional jobs as a poll-watcher, appointed to make sure that elections were properly conducted . . . . But Chicago was a tough town, where gangsters like Al Capone held sway and corruption was rife. When told that he was poll-watching on behalf of a candidate who stood for clean politics, Terkel naively asked the friend who had got him the job:

'Is Ed McGrudy clean?'
'You wanna make five bucks or dontcha?'
'I wanna make five bucks.'

In the mid-1930s Terkel worked for two of the agencies set up by the New Deal administration. On one, the Illinois Writers' Project, he was employed to write radio scripts; then he developed into an actor, at first with a politically radical group. He found a niche on radio as a villain in soap operas, appeared on television, and worked as a radio disc jockey – in which capacity his gifts as an

7 Studs Terkel: actor, disc jockey and oral historian. He lived through the American Depression and put on tape his own and others' memories of the period.

interviewer became obvious. This led on to the compilation of oral histories such as *Hard Times*, from which the remaining quotations in this section are taken.

Many of the people interviewed by Terkel recalled one of the Depression's most common sights, familiar even in the glamorous heart of the city. The Broadway theatre director and producer Herman Shumlin:

Two or three blocks along Times Square [New York], you'd see these men, silent, shuffling along in line. Getting this handout of coffee and doughnuts, dealt out from great trucks, Hearst's New York *Evening Journal*, in large letters, painted on the sides . . . . Their faces, I'd stand and watch their faces, and I'd see that flat, opaque expressionless look which spelled, for me, human disaster.

◄ **8** Unemployed man in Detroit, the capital of America's automobile industry.

Such "breadlines" might extend for blocks, as men patiently waited for something to warm and nourish them from the truck or "soup-kitchen" provided by charitable or other organizations. These were for the people who had fallen lowest, the hopeless thousands who had unwillingly joined the ranks of the hoboes, sleeping under bridges or in dosshouses. Many more who managed to keep roofs over their heads were forced to apply for relief (the American term for payments made to the needy). A former publishing house editor described it as a crucifixion, since you were subjected to a humiliating cross-examination in order to be "certified" and receive a few dollars a month. Diana Morgan, who worked in a relief office,

... found out how everybody, in order to be eligible for relief, had to have reached absolute bottom. You didn't have to have a lot of brains to realize that once they reached this stage and you put them on an allowance of a dollar a day for food – how could they ever pull out of it?

Nevertheless, there were, even then, people who believed that relief was being wasted on the worthless and workshy.

For some underprivileged groups, notably Blacks, the impact of the Depression was reduced by the fact that times had *never* been good: they had no part in the American Dream, and were not, therefore, disillusioned when it faded away. For farmers, too, the 1920s had not been boom years: farm prices had collapsed in 1921, and had never recovered. In the 1920s, banks had foreclosed on their loans and drove the farmers from their land; and in the 1930s it was more of the same. Occasionally, the farmers were able to fight back with a show of solidarity. When one of their number was sold up, recalled Harry Terrell,

all the neighbours'd come in, and they got the idea of spending twenty-five cents for a horse. They was paying ten cents for a plow. And when it was all over they'd all give it back to him.

If anyone offered realistic prices, intending to make a genuine purchase, "they would be dealt with seriously, as it were". In spite of such contrivances, large numbers of farmers left the land and became migrant workers. Their story is told by John Steinbeck, whose work is described on pages 56-9. In the 1930s, the United States was a country where millions of people were on the move in search of work. Sizeable shanty-town camps sprang up almost overnight and were deserted even more quickly when cleared by impatient authorities.

The reach of the Depression was remarkable. It was felt even by students on the campuses of American universities. The film critic Pauline Kael remembered:

When I attended Berkeley in 1936, so many of the kids [students] had actually lost their fathers. They had wandered off in disgrace because they couldn't support their families. Other fathers had killed themselves, so the family could have the insurance. Families had totally broken down. Each father took it as his personal

9 Breadline in Times Square: men queue for a handout in the sophisticated heart of New York's nightlife, while neon signs advertize theatres, night clubs and hotels.

failure . . . . It was still the Depression. There were kids who didn't have a place to sleep, huddling under bridges on the campus. I had a scholarship, but there were times when I didn't have food.

As this suggests, many American men were deeply ashamed of their "failure", despite the fact that millions were struggling with the same problems. Although Europeans shared these feelings to some extent (traditionally the man was supposed to be the "breadwinner"), Americans were much more inclined to believe that a person's material success was the measure of his personal worth. Herman Shumlin described an encounter with an old and once-prosperous friend, who tried to avoid him:

He told me that his wife had kicked him out. His children had had such contempt for him 'cause he couldn't pay the rent, he just had to leave, to get out of the house. He lived in perpetual shame. This was, to me, the most cruel thing of the Depression. Almost worse than not having food. Accepting the idea that you were just no good. No matter what you'd been before.

Anxiety and feelings of insecurity plagued many Americans during the Depression. Even

those with "good" jobs were afraid of losing them. Eileen Barth was a social worker who dealt with the jobless:

I had a terrible guilt feeling. I was living rather well, sharing a nice apartment with two other girls. My top pay was $135 a month, which made me well off. Yet there were constant layoffs. I always felt that if I lost my job I might go on relief, too. So I never really had a sense of security myself.

Employers might decide quite suddenly to lay off workers or cut their wages; or they might even go out of business altogether. Public authorities could not close down, but even they were no longer reliable. Elsa Ponselle:

I began to teach in December, 1930, and I was paid until June, 1931. When we came back [after the summer vacation], the city had gone broke . . . . My father provided me with enough money to get by. But it was another thing for the men who were married and had children.

They began to pay us with warrants, which carried six percent interest. A marvellous investment. But not for the teachers who had to take them for pay. They had to peddle those warrants for what they could get.

So shrewd businessmen made big profits on the warrants, knowing that sooner or later the city would be able to pay them off. Some stores (Elsa Ponselle: "They were wonderful") took the warrants at their face value; others accepted them only after deducting a heavy discount.

With so many people ready to do any job they could find, employers were in a strong position: in the event of trouble with the workforce they could easily find replacements. Trade union militants were dismissed as "agitators" and blacklisted, and the police were used ruthlessly to crush strikes. "Few people are aware that brutality did not start yesterday", the lawyer Max R. Naiman remarked to Studs Terkel, recalling meetings broken up, prisoners made to run a gauntlet of blows, and labour organizers beaten up and

10 A meal in a soup-kitchen. The American tradition emphasized individual self-reliance, but during the Depression many were hungry enough to accept charity.

run out of town. A retired judge, Samuel A. Heller, who had presided in the Landlord and Tenants Court, summed up even more pessimistically: "Everybody's got rights on paper. But they don't mean three cents in actual life."

In these and other respects, matters improved after 1933, when Franklin D. Roosevelt was elected president of the United States and introduced the New Deal. Most of the people who spoke to Studs Terkel praised the President and declared that they had been helped by the New Deal. But the Depression refused to go away. In 1937, just as prospects for the economy began to look brighter, there was another bad slide. Elsa Ponselle:

The Depression was a way of life for me, from the time I was twenty to the time I was thirty. I thought it was going to be for ever and ever and ever.

Finally, the war came, and – except for those killed or maimed in action – the good times were back again.

The difference was soon felt everywhere, even in the penitentiary. According to Scoop Langford, serving a life sentence, "The Depression hit that prison pretty bad. We were practically not eating." But

We fared lots better when the war was on. Food and more food, during the war. Yeah, the fellas talked about it. They said, 'Long live the war!'

Walter Greenwood (1903-74)

In Britain, the Great Depression was generally known as "the Slump". The Depression burst the bubble of American prosperity, but in Britain there was no bubble to burst: times were hard for many people during the entire period between the World Wars (1919-39), when there were never at any moment less than a million workers registered as unemployed. Here, the Slump did not create the economic crisis, although it made matters immensely worse.

Britain was still a great power, ruling over the largest empire the world had ever seen. But the foundations of her greatness were being steadily undermined. In the nineteenth century Britain had become "the Workshop of the World", the supreme financial and manufacturing nation, as a result of the first Industrial Revolution. By 1919, however, she had been weakened by the immense sacrifices made during the First World War, and her older industries were steadily declining. Most of these industries (coal, textiles, iron and steel, shipbuilding) were concentrated in the north of England, central Scotland and South Wales – heavily populated areas whose smoke-blackened towns housed long-established communities of industrial workers. And so, although the south of England and the Midlands were also hit by the Slump, in the old industrial areas the hard times began earlier and went on long after conditions elsewhere had begun to improve.

Walter Greenwood was a child of the industrial North, born and brought up in Salford, Manchester's "twin" and neighbouring city; in recent times, both have been swallowed by Greater Manchester, and even in the 1920s they were really parts of a single commercial and industrial centre. Working-class Salford, lightly fictionalized, is the setting of Greenwood's novel *Love on the Dole*, which is recognized as a classic account of

11 Walter Greenwood, whose novel *Love on the Dole* drew attention to the plight of the unemployed in Britain's northern industrial towns.

12 Grim rows of back-to-back houses. Millions of these had been crammed together during the nineteenth century to accommodate the masses of workers imported from the country to work in the booming factories. But by the 1920s the houses were old and the factories no longer booming.

northern poverty and endurance. Greenwood had observed most of the things he wrote about, had held a variety of jobs without ever earning more that £1.15s. a week, and had stood in dole queues on many occasions. Paradoxically, *Love on the Dole* was such a success that it liberated him from the very way of life he described.

This was, at best, hard and unlovely. Its setting was a blackened landscape, "millions of chimneys exhaling simultaneously; smoke drifting, converging, hanging, an immense pall over the Two Cities." Beneath,

jungles of tiny houses cramped and huddled together, the cradles of generations of the future. Places whose men and women are born, live, love and die and pay preposterous rents for the privilege of calling the grimy houses 'home'.

Overcrowded places, where brothers and sisters share a bed, or sleep in the same room as their parents. A cold, rainy city where work starts early: at 5.30 a.m. a man carrying a long pole tipped with wires clatters down the street in his clogs, rattling the wires against bedroom windows to rouse their inmates. In Greenwood's fictional Hankey Park the men work at the local engineering factory, while their sisters and daughters are employed at the textile mills. If it is a Monday morning, the wives are soon queuing outside the pawnbroker's with their bundles, "a crush of unwashed women, hair tumbled, come to raise the wind [get some cash] so that they might have money to spend on food". Suits, wedding rings and other valuables are "popped" each Monday and redeemed on Friday night or Saturday, after the wage-earners have been paid. Even so, many people are in debt, and solvency means being able to keep up payments to the insurance collectors and "clothing club" (hire purchase) representatives who call every Saturday. Only the employed young men and girls can afford a few cheap luxuries – stockings and short skirts, a dance and cinema show – before marriage, responsibilities and poverty make them old before their time.

Harry Hardcastle, the central character in

Love on the Dole, has just finished school; his father is a miner, his mother "an old woman of forty". Fascinated by the powerful machinery and male camaraderie of Marlowe's engineering works, Harry signs indentures to become an apprentice. He gradually discovers that Larry Meath, a young socialist workman, is right about "the apprentice racket": for seven years he will provide Marlowe's with cheap labour; he will learn almost nothing, since technology has reduced "engineering" to simple machine-minding; and when his seven years are up, Marlowe's will fire him, taking on fresh "apprentices" rather than pay a full adult wage. As he sees the older apprentices become street-loungers, and finds himself in charge of new, younger boys, Harry understands:

Every year new generations of schoolboys were appearing, each generation pushing him and his a little nearer to that incredible abyss of manhood and the dole.

This was a daunting prospect in times when "trade" was bad; and that seemed to mean all the time, although every three months or so the newspapers ran headlines saying "Prosperity in sight. Trade turning the corner." However, by the time Harry becomes a qualified engineer – and is sacked – the Slump is under way, and conditions are far worse. Now even "safe" jobs are under threat, and skilled men such as Larry Meath (who had hesitated to marry Harry's sister, Sally, on his £2.5s. a week) find themselves in the dole queue alongside exploited "apprentices" like Harry.

Harry Hardcastle, white mercerized cotton scarf wrapped loosely about his neck, a tuft of fair hair protruding from beneath the neb [peak] of his oily cap, patches on the knees and backside of his overalls, stood in a long queue of shabby men, hands in pockets, staring fixedly and unseeing at the ground. At street corners, leaning against house walls or squatting on the kerbstones, were more men, clothes stinking of age, waiting until the queue opposite went into the building when they would take their places in

13 and 14 The unemployed march to demand justice (top), but come into conflict with the police (bottom). Two dramatic scenes from the film of *Love on the Dole*.

forming another. And all through the day, every quarter-hour, would see another crowd of fresh faces coming to sign the unemployed register at their appointed times.

Inside the labour exchange there are new queues, followed by a tedious ritual of "musical chairs" as claimants move towards the pay counter. The only place where business is done briskly and quickly is at the counter under the Situations Vacant sign, since jobs are virtually non-existent. Harry, desperate to find employment so that he can marry his pregnant girlfriend, hopes "it was true what the papers and people said about these fellows. Perhaps these fellows never looked for work, didn't want it." But when he himself looks he is soon disillusioned, and over the next few months succumbs to the demoralizing effects of unemployment.

It got you slowly, with the slippered stealth of an unsuspected malignant disease.

You fell into the habit of slouching, of putting your hands into your pockets and keeping them there; of glancing at people, furtively, ashamed of your secret, until you fancied that everybody eyed you with suspicion. You knew that your shabbiness betrayed you; it was apparent for all to see. You prayed for the winter evenings and the kindly darkness. Darkness, poverty's cloak. Breeches backside patched and repatched; patches on knees, on elbows. Jesus! All bloody patches. Gor' blimey! . . .

Nothing to do with time; nothing to spend; nothing to do tomorrow nor the day after; nothing to wear; can't get married. A living corpse; a unit of the spectral army of three million lost men.

Worse is to follow. The government cuts the dole twice, first of all directly, and then by imposing a "means test" (see page 23). During a protest march Larry Meath is killed when police charge the crowd with truncheons flailing. Sally Hardcastle, all her hopes broken, becomes the mistress of the local bookmaker, who uses his influence to get jobs for Harry and his father. For employed and unemployed alike, life goes on in Hankey Park.

Ivar Kreuger (1880-1932)

The poor were not the only victims of the Depression. Many businessmen, large and small, were ruined by the slump in share values or its economic consequences. People who had lived comfortably on dividends from investments were also brought low. In her autobiography, *Twopence to Cross the Mersey* (1974), Helen Forrester recalled her muddled youthful realization that

Father had done a mysterious thing called 'going bankrupt', a not uncommon occurrence in the world of 1930, but strange to me. I had heard vaguely that going bankrupt was an American disease which had struck Wall Street in New York, and that Americans committed suicide when this happened to them; mentally, I saw dozens of them hurling themselves off the tops of skyscrapers, and I wondered where Father would find a skyscraper.

What actually happened was that the Forresters started life again in Depression-struck Liverpool. With less experience of poverty than most working-class people, they were barely able to cope, and Helen Forrester's book gives a painfully graphic account of their wretched, verminous existence.

Helen Forrester was not alone in believing that large numbers of suicidal Americans were flinging themselves from skyscrapers; this became one of the most firmly established Depression myths. In reality, there were only a few suicides, most of whom chose less dramatic methods of ending their lives. Some despaired because they were ruined; others because they faced long prison sentences. People who had committed business frauds and similar crimes constituted a tiny minority, but there were some sensational examples during the Depression. One effect of the Crash was to show up any kind of dishonest dealing, either because embezzlers lost in speculation the money they had "borrowed" from their companies, or because a corporate bankruptcy was followed by a thorough examination of a firm's books. Among those who parted with fortunes on Wall Street were the principal officers of the Union Industrial Bank of Flint, Michigan. The fortunes, however, belonged to the bank, and the trial and conviction of the officers was a major scandal. Richard Whitney, a former president of the New York Stock Exchange, represented a different kind of criminal – one who, through pride or cowardice, refused to face up to bankruptcy, raising bigger and bigger loans in a desperate attempt to keep going, and eventually committing illegalities that came to light when a smash could no longer be avoided. In the case of Whitney, this meant obtaining loans on the security of stocks and bonds that he passed off as his own property, although they actually belonged to his clients.

Both kinds of criminality were practised by Ivar Kreuger, the Swedish "Match King". Kreuger was the most spectacular of all the Depression's victims, an internationally renowned financier who dealt in hundreds of millions of pounds, negotiated on equal terms with national governments, and was quoted with respect by the world's leading economists. When he shot himself in his Paris flat on 12 March 1932, the media blamed Kreuger's death on the strain of conducting his great enterprises during a world depression. In Britain, *The Times* noted that "least of all does personal suspicion light on him", while the *Economist* hailed him as "a man of great constructive intelligence". But within a few weeks, once qualified accountants had investigated his affairs, Kreuger was being denounced as a swindler and a counterfeiter.

Ivar Kreuger was the son of a match manufacturer, and his native country was one of the traditional centres of match production. Nevertheless, he trained as an engineer and first made his reputation by pioneering the use of reinforced concrete in Sweden. It was only during the First World War that he began to show his genius as a financier and organizer, masterminding the amalgamations that created a single Swedish Match Company, with Kreuger himself as its president.

Kreuger realized that although matches were among the cheapest of everyday objects, they were also indispensable – and used on a scale that could make them very big business

◀ **15** Ivar Kreuger, the Swedish 'Match King', at his headquarters, the 'Match Palace' in Stockholm.

indeed. In the 1920s he set out to control the world's match production. With a highly profitable business behind him, and the bankers in Sweden and the United States eager to provide additional finance, he began to buy up match factories all over the world, from Belgium to Japan. Most of these operations were carried out in secret, so that Kreuger's competitors failed to realize what was happening until it was too late. But his public coups were equally impressive. By making large loans to European governments in return for monopolistic concessions, Kreuger became an internationally admired figure. War-devastated Europe desperately needed capital, and Kreuger performed a real public service by providing it, mainly with cash that he had himself borrowed from the United States. In France, where a timely Kreuger loan had averted an economic crisis, he was awarded the coveted Légion d'Honneur and saluted as "the saviour of Europe".

In the course of the 1920s Kreuger achieved control of three-quarters of the world's match production. He also moved into new industries and eventually manipulated the destinies of about 400 companies and banks. Hardly anyone grasped the fragility of Kreuger's empire, which rested on his ability to raise huge loans and keep his shareholders happy by declaring large dividends. His real resources were considerable, but he regularly exaggerated them in order to float new share issues and borrow yet more money. Funds were siphoned from one Kreuger company to another, or in and out of Kreuger's pockets, without any effective control by boards of directors or accountants; and the financial statements issued by the Match King himself were dazzling but vague as to details, leaving nobody the wiser. Only Kreuger really knew what was going on in his 400 companies and how they related to one another; and he kept

16 Kreuger's suicide, although put down to overwork, created a new financial panic — even before the full truth was known. ▶

the information locked inside his undoubtedly brilliant brain. For years he was able to fend off awkward enquiries by pleading the need for secrecy in the kind of delicate, high-level operations he conducted. There were surprisingly few enquirers, and they were easily satisfied, partly because Kreuger was successful but also because he was a man of mesmeric personality. Even many years after the collapse of his empire, a colleague remembered him with awe:

There was an odd air of greatness about Ivar. I think he could get people to do anything. They fell for him, they couldn't resist his charm and magnetism.

By the late 1920s Kreuger had become dangerously over-ambitious, expanding at a tremendous rate with borrowed money. However, the supply of American dollars seemed limitless, and it can be argued that, but for the Depression, the profits from Kreuger's empire would eventually have paid off his borrowings. Confidence in the Match King was so strong that he weathered the 1929 Crash and even floated new loans; but as the Depression went on and on, money grew tighter, and even Kreuger was unable to prevent a slide in the value of his holdings. Growing desperate, he began to speculate heavily on the Wall Street Stock Exchange, hoping to benefit from an upturn in the market. Instead, the market continued to fall, and the once infallible Kreuger lost millions. By early 1932 he was multiplying lies and evasions, and even stooped to outright criminality by counterfeiting Italian state bonds to the value of £28 million. Finally, as new payments fell due and his creditors closed in, Ivar Kreuger was faced with death or disgrace and imprisonment, and made his choice.

◀ **17** Children, too, endured hard times and squalor in Depression-hit towns such as Liverpool, as Helen Forrester's book *Twopence to Cross the Mersey* recounts.

WITNESS AND PROTEST

Wal Hannington (1895-1966) and Ellen Wilkinson (1891-1947)

There were some vociferous protests against poverty and unemployment in Britain during the 1920s and 1930s, though they made only a limited impact on the predominantly Conservative governments of the time. In 1921 a National Unemployed Workers' Movement (NUWM) was founded by Wal Hannington, a skilful propagandist who organized several spectacular "hunger marches" on London from the distressed areas

18 Wal Hannington, Communist organizer of the National Unemployed Workers' Movement.

and argued forcefully for better treatment of the unemployed. The NUWM was not recognized by the TUC or the Labour Party, whose official leaderships were intent on becoming respectable and accepted: the militancy of the movement, and the Communist affiliations of Hannington and most of the other NUWM activists, were seen as positive embarrassments. Whether a more militant Labour Party attitude would have changed anything is, of course, impossible to know.

Labour was nominally the party of government in 1929-31, when the Depression hit Britain. At this time there was a "hung Parliament", in which none of the three main parties had an overall majority in the House of Commons; the Labour Government was able to survive only with Liberal support. Despite Labour's theoretical commitment to a socialist economy, its leaders held orthodox economic ideas and had no constructive policy for dealing with unemployment. And in 1931, when the financial collapse in Austria and Germany triggered a British financial crisis, Labour's prime minister, Ramsay MacDonald, and other leading cabinet ministers became convinced that only the traditional remedy – reduced public spending, including a cut in the dole – could "save the pound". The Labour Party split on the issue, and in August 1931 MacDonald and a few of his colleagues joined forces with the Conservatives and Liberals to form a "National" Government. As a result, down to the Second World War Britain was ruled by a succession of governments that were technically "National" and in practice predominantly Conservative, with the Labour Party in permanent opposition.

The economies that were made to defend the pound included the imposition of higher taxes to raise revenue, combined with cuts in the wages paid to public employees such as civil servants, policemen, teachers and members of the armed forces. In some sectors, notably teaching, the cuts were resisted and modified; and after a naval mutiny at Invergordon – news of which was carefully suppressed – the new rates for the forces were hastily revised.

Most of the cuts amounted to roughly 10 per cent of the wages and salaries involved. But the poorest people – the unemployed – were made to suffer far more. This was partly because the payment of unemployment insurance benefit ("dole") was the largest single item on the government's "wage" bill (by August 1931 there were 2,700,000 unemployed), and partly perhaps because the unemployed were the section of the community least capable of fighting back effectively. To begin with, most married women were deprived of benefit, and the dole itself was cut by roughly 10 per cent, so that a married man with two children, who had been receiving £1.10s. a week, was now given only £1.7s.3d. Since £1.10s. was only sufficient to sustain the most meagre, unhealthy standard of living, the cut was bad enough in itself; but worse was to follow. After 26 weeks' unemployment, the insured worker lost his (or her) right to receive benefit automatically, and was "means tested". The household in which the worker lived was investigated, and his dole might be reduced or cut off completely if any extra family income existed that might be used towards supporting him. Items such as a father's pension, or the earnings or savings of a brother or sister, were considered as elements in a collective household income which might be deemed adequate to support all its members – in which case the unemployed man's dole was cut off without any right of appeal. Thus the unemployed person became a charge on his or her relatives, whose incentive to better themselves was weakened by the knowledge that any increase in their wages would simply mean that an equivalent amount would be knocked off the dole money coming into the house. One of the curious results of this measure, introduced by conservative-minded politicians, was to break up family life. The employed girl saving to get married was better off in lodgings than at home, where she was forced to support her unemployed brother; alternatively, the unemployed person, by leaving, qualified for the full dole allowance and ceased to be a burden on the family household.

The Means Test was hated because it involved a humiliating inquisition into a family's affairs. Furthermore, when it had been done and the unemployed person had been assessed, he or she was no longer paid unemployment insurance benefit, but a new "transitional benefit" which varied from place to place but almost always made the recipient even worse off than before. However, many of the locally appointed committees (Public Assistance Committees, or PACs) that administered the Means Test were surprisingly sympathetic to the unemployed, and bent or broke the regulations to help them. The subsequent history of the Means Test was a tangled one, with the government attempting to impose a lower national rate against a long-drawn-out rearguard action by the PACs, the NUWM and concerned MPs, by no means all of them representing the Labour Party.

During the 1930s, Hannington continued to organize hunger marches and demonstrations against the Means Test. The NUWM was also behind local actions to help specific groups. One well-known incident occurred in September 1932, when a mass demonstration pressured the Birkenhead PAC into raising its transitional benefit for a man from a beggarly 12s. to 15s. However, the demonstrators clashed with the police as they were marching away, and four days of sporadic fighting followed. The members of the NUWM, seen as "Reds" with no influential friends, were easily victimized, since they had no access to the newspapers,

19 and 20 Police in action against demonstrators in 1930 and 1931. The photographs give quite different impressions of the role played by the police, showing how false is the saying 'the camera never lies'.

radio or newsreels, which largely ignored their activities. Though a certain amount was achieved by the NUWM, its lack of respectability told against it.

The reverse was true of the Jarrow March, which has become one of the great legends of the 1930s. It was a consciously respectable, non-political march, given wide and sympathetic media coverage, that achieved nothing tangible and yet looms large in all the histories of the period.

Jarrow is a town on Tyneside, a part of the north-east coast of England whose chief industries were shipbuilding, coal mining and the manufacture of steel. All of these had been declining since 1918, making Tyneside one of the "distressed areas" in which the full severity of the Depression continued to be felt throughout the 1930s.

Jarrow itself was one of the hardest hit towns in the whole country, for its prosperity had been based on the activities of a single firm, Palmers the shipbuilders. With the industry in the doldrums, the great shipbuilding companies had formed a combine – an organization in which they co-operated to keep up prices and reduce the number of existing firms so that there were more orders for those that remained. As part of this process, known as "rationalization", in 1934 Palmers was bought up and put out of business. The shipbuilders' combine was so determined to prevent any revival in Jarrow that the site and stock of the firm were sold with the stipulation that they were not to be used for shipbuilding over a 40-year period.

The effect on Jarrow was catastrophic. By 1936 only 1300 people had jobs in a town with a population of 35,000. Just what it meant for an entire town to be on the dole was shown in statistics: Jarrow's death rate was one of the highest in Britain, and the number of tuberculosis cases was twice the national average. For two years the townspeople hoped that the setting up of a steel works might solve their worst problem, but the Iron and Steel Federation – another combine – sabotaged the proposal because the Federation, too, was intent on restricting competition and "rationalizing" the industry. Finally, the

21 Ellen Wilkinson, the diminutive Labour MP for Jarrow, with some of the Jarrow marchers and the petition they carried with them to Parliament.

President of the Board of Trade, Walter Runciman, announced the government's attitude: "Jarrow must work out its own salvation."

This was, of course, impossible, and the Jarrow council and the town's Labour MP, Ellen Wilkinson, made plans for a more forceful appeal to the government. Ellen Wilkinson, a tiny, fiery, red-haired left-winger, was variously known as "Red Ellen", "Our Ellen" and "the Mighty Atom". She had only been MP for Jarrow since the general election of 1935, but she had considerable earlier experience of the fight against unemployment. She had worked closely with Wal Hannington and, like him, believed that "as long as the unemployed keep quiet and starve, nothing will be done for them". Legend has made Ellen Wilkinson the inspirer and leader of the Jarrow March, but in fact the main decisions were taken by the town councillors. When it was decided to hold a march on London Ellen Wilkinson suggested that the Jarrow contingent might join the forthcoming NUWM hunger march; but the idea was turned down. A hunger march (that is, a protest against the near-starvation caused by the dole regulations) was implicitly a criticism of government policy; the "Jarrow Crusade" would be a respectful request for government help, backed by all shades of political opinion in the town. Two hundred of Jarrow's fittest unemployed men were selected to march the 300 miles to London and present a petition with 11,000 signatures, praying

that HM Government realize the urgent need for providing work for the town without further delay, actively assist resuscitation of industry, and render such other actions as may be meet.

On 5 October 1936 the Jarrow men set out, with a mouth-organ band playing merrily at the front. Each man was equipped with a groundsheet, which in good weather could be carried across the chest, like a sash, and was transformed into a cape when it rained. The marchers were a small, well-disciplined group, and their cheerful temper and good behaviour made a favourable impression everywhere they went. Thanks to excellent forward planning and Jarrow's non-political approach, even comfortable Conservative towns such as Harrogate welcomed the

22 Jarrow men marching to a tune played by a mouth organ band.

marchers with sympathetic hospitality – so much so that the men's health improved noticeably. Councils and political organizations arranged accommodation for them, and at Leicester the cobblers of the Co-operative Society worked all night to mend their shoes. The leader of the march, the burly, bowler-hatted Councillor David Riley, remarked: "I never thought that there was so much generosity and good nature in the world."

The media, which had ignored the NUWM's marches, gave the Jarrow Crusade very favourable publicity. The flamboyant presence of Ellen Wilkinson also attracted the media, although her participation was interrupted by political duties (and, probably, by sheer physical frailty). Among the duties was a speech at the Labour Party Conference in which she tried to obtain official backing for the marchers:

I tell the Executive that they are missing the most marvellous opportunity of a generation. The March of Jarrow is a great folk movement. What propaganda speech is equal to that vast object lesson of the town that was murdered in the interests of the Stock Exchange and rationalization?

Ironically, the Jarrow Crusade has entered the folk memory, and has become identified with the Labour Party – yet in October 1936 the Party refused Ellen Wilkinson's appeal for endorsement, evidently fearing that it might be compromised if some Communist participation came to light.

On the last day of October the Crusade entered London in a heavy downpour. Londoners made them welcome, but the Bishop of Durham denounced them for trying to put "unconstitutional" pressure on the Government. Ministers were hostile, and refused to meet the marchers. Ellen Wilkinson told a huge rally in Hyde Park:

Do not wonder that this cabinet does not want to see us. It does not want anybody to tell the truth about these black areas in the North, in Scotland, and in South Wales, that have been left to rot.

Ellen Wilkinson presented Jarrow's petition at the Bar of the House of Commons, and spoke on behalf of her constituents. The petition received cursory attention, and then the House moved on to other matters. The Mayor and the marchers held a meeting inside the Houses of Parliament that was attended by many MPs; then – rejecting the idea of a sit-in – they left and caught a train back to Jarrow.

Nothing was done for the town by the Government, although a couple of small factories were opened by private business concerns. It is possible that the Jarrow Crusade altered general attitudes in the long run, but in material terms the NUWM hunger march which reached London was more successful: it was met by the Minister of Labour, who did make some concessions concerning the introduction of new dole regulations. Yet it is the Jarrow March that the world remembers.

Ellen Wilkinson, in her book *The Town That Was Murdered* (1939), claims only that the march kept up people's spirits. Arguably, her own great achievement of the 1930s was the Hire Purchase Act of 1939. During the Depression, the only way millions of people could buy clothes, furniture, radios and similar goods was by hire purchase; but, without realizing it, they were often made to pay exorbitant amounts of interest on the goods, which could be reclaimed by the hire purchase company if they fell behind with their payments. Ellen Wilkinson's Act compelled the trader to display the interest charges clearly, and laid down that people who fell behind but had made a third of the total payments could not be automatically deprived of their goods; instead, a court of law could arrange a new, lighter schedule of payments. The Act did not give Ellen Wilkinson everything she wanted, but it did provide some protection for millions of poor people. Though overshadowed by the Jarrow Crusade, it was a major reform of the Depression era.

William L. Shirer (1904-   )

The Depression affected the lives of all sorts of people, including the distinguished foreign correspondents of newspapers. The American journalist William L. Shirer had begun his career in Paris and had made his mark by reporting events from the great European capitals for the *Chicago Tribune*. In 1930, while based in Vienna, he was sent to India in order to cover the progress of Gandhi's civil disobedience campaign against British rule. He carried out the assignment, cabled good stories from the Middle East on his way back, returned to Vienna in the autumn of 1932 – and was fired. The excuse given by the *Tribune* was unconvincing, and as he relates in his autobiography, *The Nightmare Years*, Shirer was bewildered: "Only later did I realize that probably I was just another casualty of the Depression, one of the millions."

23 William L. Shirer (seated) with another famous American foreign correspondent, Ed Murrow.

It turned out that the *Tribune*'s proprietor was drastically cutting down on staff employed abroad, and that other American newspapers were doing the same. And for that reason Shirer's prospects looked bleak:

I quickly found out that it would not be easy to find another job in Europe. As the Depression deepened at home, the few newspapers that had a foreign staff . . . and all three American news agencies, also were cutting down. I telephoned their European chiefs in London or Paris. They said they would keep me in mind. But for the moment they were not having any correspondents.

Luckily for Shirer, he had managed to save a thousand dollars over the previous five years. He had just married and was not too unhappy to take a year off. He and his wife would go to Spain – a poor country where living was amazingly cheap – and sit out the Depression; if Shirer succeeded in making a new career as a writer, so much the better. But even this plan was jeopardized by the Depression, since the United States went off the Gold Standard, which ensured a fixed value for the dollar, and the Shirers suddenly found their savings worth 40 per cent less than they had been a few weeks before. However, Spain proved even cheaper than Shirer had anticipated, and he was still able to take his year off. But, at the end of it, the Depression had not eased and Shirer had not established himself as a writer. As their money ran out in the winter of 1933-4, the Shirers wrapped themselves in blankets because they couldn't afford fuel, and they stopped eating meat, which was expensive. Shirer made frantic attempts to find a job, and eventually succeeded: he was appointed to take over the copy-desk of the American Paris *Herald*. Though cheered by the prospect of working in the French capital, Shirer inevitably felt unhappy about doing a relatively mundane job, processing other men's stories:

This was a comedown of course. After six years as a foreign correspondent in Europe and Asia I would be returning to where I started nearly nine years before: on the copy-desk of an American newspaper in Paris. That was progress? The thought depressed me. But, like everyone else, we had to eat.

As it turned out, Shirer had returned at a moment of crisis, and his services as a reporter were called on almost immediately. When he returned in January 1934 he found that "Paris and France had changed and, like my own life, for the worse. I scarcely recognized them." Politically, France had long been unstable, with governments rising and falling every few months because there were many political parties and no single one of them ever commanded a majority of seats in the Chamber of Deputies (Parliament). In spite of this, from the mid-1920s France had been prosperous, and political antagonisms had seemed relatively mild.

By January 1934, all this had changed. Following the financial crises of 1931 in Austria, Germany and Britain, share prices collapsed on the Bourse (Paris Stock Exchange), and France, too, suffered from falling industrial production and a soaring rate of unemployment. Shirer noted that

The Depression was never quite as bad in France as in more industrialized Germany, Britain and the United States. Unemployment seldom rose above half a million. But the slump was bad enough, the worst economic and financial crisis the country had experienced in more than a hundred years.

French governments reacted feebly to the crisis, like most governments between 1929 and 1933. But if France's rulers were not actually much worse than the others, they *looked* worse, thanks to France's political instability and a series of financial scandals that threatened to discredit the entire republican system. All followed much the same pattern:

Crooks, with the aid of bribed cabinet members, senators and deputies, were able to set up in

24 The Depression hits Paris: a queue outside the municipal soup-kitchen in the rue Réaumur.

business, including banking, and then, when they were caught, evade trial or have their cases continually postponed or the charges quashed, sometimes by the minister of justice himself, who was in on the deal.

In this atmosphere of economic depression and political disillusion, extreme right-wing groups – hostile to any kind of parliamentary system – flourished. These were either royalist, like Action Française, or more or less conscious imitations of the Italian Fascist or German Nazi parties, financed and sometimes led by business tycoons such as the electrical magnate Ernest Mercier or the famous perfumier François Coty. Like their Italian and German counterparts, they denounced parliamentary government as weak and corrupt, and promised to restore law, order and stability.

When Shirer arrived in Paris the biggest scandal of all had just come to light. Serge Stavisky was a swindler on the grand scale, dealing in hundreds of millions of francs, owning newspapers of varying political persuasions, and building up an impressive network of influential and respectable friends and colleagues. He had been accused of a serious fraud as far back as 1927, but with the

help of his "friends" he had managed to have his trial postponed on no less than 19 occasions! Meanwhile, he had created a financial empire – which collapsed on Christmas Eve 1933, when it became apparent that 239 million francs' worth of municipal bonds, issued by the city of Bayonne and guaranteed by Stavisky, were worthless. Stavisky himself fled, but was traced to a villa at Chamonix where he shot himself on 8 January, before the police broke in . . . . Or so it was said: many Frenchmen believed that Stavisky's pursuers had murdered him rather than see him stand trial and implicate leading police officers, newspaper editors and politicians in his crimes. And it does seem certain that, at the very least, no attempt was made to save his life, so that he bled to death without medical assistance.

To the enemies of the republic this seemed an ideal opportunity to overthrow it. The scandal was all the juicier because relatives of the prime minister had been involved with Stavisky, while the fact that Stavisky himself was Russian-born and Jewish could be used to appeal to deep-seated prejudices among ordinary Frenchmen. The first serious riots were launched by Action Française on 9 January. They carried on, night after night, even after the Government gave in and resigned. The new government, led by Edouard Daladier, seemed determined to thoroughly investigate the Stavisky affair and maintain order. But the riots went on, and their political backing became obvious as the cry "Hang the Deputies!" was more and more frequently heard. The climax occurred on the night of 6 February, when thousands of royalists, fascists and Communists assembled in the Place de la Concorde, and tried to storm the Chamber of Deputies just across the river. They were faced by the police and the Garde Mobile, a mounted security force armed with sabres. Shirer joined other reporters on the balcony of the Hotel Crillon and watched the pitched battle that followed. Among the reporters was a woman he didn't know:

The first shots we didn't hear. Suddenly the woman slumped silently to the floor. When we

25 Ruins of a barricade stormed by the police during the Stavisky riots.

bent over her, blood was flowing from her face from a bullet hole in the centre of her forehead. She was dead.

The firing became general, and the battle raged for hours, until the almost exhausted *gendarmes* and Garde Mobile managed to clear the square with a last determined charge. The casualty list was a long one: the police and Garde Mobile lost one man dead and 1664 wounded, while 16 rioters were killed and 665 injured.

Mysteriously, the largest of the fascist organizations, the Croix de Feu, had not joined the rioters, apparently because their chief lost his nerve. This may well have made all the difference between the survival and the destruction of the republic. As it was, Daladier was pressured into resigning, but the next government managed to weather the storm. France, unlike neighbouring Germany, remained a democracy, although her weakened and demoralized political system proved ill-equipped to deal with the expansionist policies of the Third Reich.

Shirer was to witness the history of Nazi Germany from 1934 to 1940 at first hand, since in August 1934 he was offered a foreign correspondent's job in Berlin. He would later build on both his French and his German experiences, writing two widely praised histories, *The Collapse of the Third Republic* and *The Rise and Fall of the Third Reich*. However, by the time Shirer reached Berlin the Nazis had already been in power for 18 months. It was not he, but a young English novelist, who spent the bleakest years of the German Depression in the German capital.

Christopher Isherwood (1904-1986)

Although Britain's economic problems had begun years before the Depression struck, they were mild by comparison with the crises faced by Germany between 1918 and 1933. After the wartime blockade had reduced many of the population to near-starvation, the Kaiser (German Emperor) was dethroned, and a democratic republic – the Weimar Republic – proclaimed. The treaty of Versailles which followed the German defeat, condemned German "war-guilt" and stipulated that the Germans must pay huge reparations to their former enemies. In 1923, when the Germans failed to keep up their payments, French troops occupied the Ruhr Valley, provoking a German economic collapse. The mark fell to a third of a thousand-billionth of its 1913 value as a runaway inflation made prices and wages soar. Eventually the mark was stabilized, but terrible damage had been done. In the long term, perhaps the worst-hit section of society was the middle class, whose savings had been wiped out. (If the cost of living rises from one to one million, you may be no worse off if your wages have also risen from one to one million; but your life's savings of, say, 50 have become worthless. This is what economists mean when they say that inflation hits savings and fixed incomes.)

Although the crisis of 1923 created a large group of dangerously embittered people, in subsequent years it seemed likely that the Weimar Republic would overcome its difficulties. International tensions relaxed, reparations payments were reduced and rescheduled, and with the help of American loans the economy began to thrive. Then, as we have seen, the American Depression started to have an impact on Central Europe, with shattering economic and political results.

The last years of the Weimar Republic were

witnessed at first hand by the young British writer Christopher Isherwood, who lived in Berlin from November 1929 to May 1933, and later utilized his experiences in writing two famous works of fiction, *Mr Norris Changes Trains* (1935) and *Goodbye to Berlin* (1939). In his autobiography, *Christopher and His Kind* (1977), Isherwood states frankly that as a homosexual he was attracted to Berlin because of the sexual opportunities it offered. In Germany, as in Britain, homosexuals were outlawed, but the atmosphere of the capital itself was permissive – if only because tourist Berlin thrived on its reputation for "decadence" and sophisticated nightlife;

◀ **26** The novelist Christopher Isherwood (left) with his close friend, the poet W.H. Auden.

27 Inflation in Germany. With prices soaring and paper money almost worthless, the till of this shop is no longer big enough to hold the cash, which is stuffed into tea chests.
▼

indeed, it is the combination of raffish characters and a deadly serious political and economic situation that gives Isherwood's "Berlin" books their potency.

Isherwood was not primarily a political being, and it was only after a visit from an English friend – a committed Communist – that

Christopher became increasingly aware of the kind of world he was living in. Here was the seething brew of history in the making – a brew that would test the truth of all political theories, just as actual cooking tests the cookery books. The Berlin brew seethed with unemployment, malnutrition, stock market panic, hatred of the Versailles Treaty and other potent ingredients. (*Christopher and His Kind*)

Not very long afterwards, Isherwood moved into a slum tenement (for romantic, not political, reasons) and gained some insight into the lives of the poor. A family of five lived in a flat consisting of a living room, one bedroom, and a tiny kitchen; there were two double beds in the living room, and most of the family were only too pleased to take in a lodger who could pay regularly. The flat was always too hot or too cold, the sink stank, the ceiling let in water and there was only one lavatory to every four flats. Conditions were so bad that the council had declared the flat unfit for human habitation – but couldn't find the family anywhere else to live.

Isherwood soon moved away into an area that was middle class, although badly run down, with streets of "houses like monumental safes crammed with the tarnished valuables and second-hand furniture of a bankrupt middle class". His landlady, Fraulein Thurau (fictionalized as Fraulein Schroeder, one of Isherwood's most engaging characters), was one of those who had suffered:

Like many thousands of other middle-class victims of the inflation, Frl Thurau had known wealthier days and still felt a sour amusement at finding herself forced to do menial, unladylike work. (*Christopher and His Kind*)

28 Berlin: a hectic nightlife catered for all classes and tastes.

Meanwhile, unemployment soared as the Depression took hold, and

morning after morning, all over the immense, damp dreary town and the packing-case colonies of huts in the suburb allotments, young men were waking up to another workless, empty day to be spent as they could best contrive; selling bootlaces, begging, playing draughts in the hall of the Labour Exchange, hanging about urinals, opening the doors of cars, helping with crates in the markets, gossiping, lounging, stealing, overhearing racing tips, sharing stumps of cigarette ends picked up in the gutter, singing folk songs for groschen [pennies] . . . (*Mr Norris Changes Trains*)

From time to time there were new jolts – for example, when a big bank failed:

In the middle of the door was fixed a small notice, beautifully printed in Gothic type, like a page from a classic author. The notice said that the Reichspresident had guaranteed the deposits. Everything was quite all right. Only the bank wasn't going to open. (*Goodbye to Berlin*)

As the crisis deepened, large numbers of people turned to political parties that promised radical changes. A new, militant right-wing party had emerged: the Nazi Party, which blamed Jews, Communists, Versailles and the Weimar Republic for Germany's troubles. By 1932 it was the biggest German party in terms of election votes and seats in the Reichstag (parliament), though it failed to win an outright majority. On the other wing, the Communists were also gaining votes. To Isherwood, as to many upper-class British intellectuals, shaken by the failure of "their" system, communism was doubly attractive, since it appeared to be creating a new society in the Soviet Union, while in Europe and elsewhere Communists seemed to be the most wholehearted enemies of fascism. Though Isherwood never quite committed himself to the Party, and later claimed to have spotted the "seamy side" of German Communism, *Mr Norris Changes Trains* paints a highly flattering portrait of a Communist leader, and idealizes the working-class audiences at Communist meetings. ("Their passion, their strength elated me.")

29 Berlin: 60,000 German Communists parade in military style.

The Communists, like the Nazis, hoped to destroy the Weimar Republic and set up a regime of their own. With such powerful enemies on both the Left and the Right, the pro-Weimar parties could only have formed stable governments by sinking their differences. Since they failed to do so, one election followed another, while on the streets violence between rival private armies became the norm:

Berlin was in a state of civil war. Hate exploded suddenly, without warning, out of nowhere . . . knives were whipped out, blows were dealt with spiked rings, beer-mugs, chair legs or leaded clubs . . . . In the middle of a crowded street a young man would be attacked, stripped, thrashed and left bleeding on the pavement; in fifteen seconds it was all over and the assailants had disappeared. (*Mr Norris Changes Trains*)

In the elections of November 1932 the Nazis had their first setback, losing two million votes; it is probably significant that the polling occurred at a time when the number of unemployed had fallen. But while Isherwood and his friends rejoiced, believing that the tide had turned, intrigues among right-wing politicians led, on 30 January 1933, to the formation of a coalition government with Hitler at its head. This was all that the Nazi leader needed: his hands were on the levers of power and would not be removed during his lifetime. A fire at the Reichstag on 27 February was blamed on the Communists, and mass arrests began. Soon, using its own state institutions, the Nazis would destroy the Weimar Republic by outlawing all political parties except Hitler's, suppressing the trade unions and making newspapers and radio the mouthpieces of a new state: the Third Reich. Even by May 1933, when Isherwood left Germany, most of his friends were in prison, had "disappeared", or had gone into exile. He was not to witness the way in which Hitler, after his own fashion, ended the Depression in Germany.

SAVIOURS

John Maynard Keynes (1883-1946)

In the 1920s, British governments based their financial and industrial policies on orthodox economic theories. The fundamental assumptions of these theories had scarcely changed since the nineteenth century, when Britain was "the Workshop of the World", easily out-producing other countries. This situation encouraged economists to believe in *laissez faire* – the doctrine that governments should not interfere with the operation of "market forces" in trade and industry. Left to itself, competition would produce maximum efficiency and social benefit; competition between businessmen, for example, would force them to market their wares as efficiently as possible, so that they might sell more cheaply than their rivals could – to the benefit of the consumer. The laws of supply, demand and pricing could be left to operate automatically, since the entire system was self-adjusting; for example, if the supply of any item increased, its price would fall until it became attractive enough to create the increased demand needed to absorb the supply. The same rules were supposed to govern labour: if the supply of the labour exceeded the demand – that is, if there was unemployment – the price of labour (wages and salaries) would fall, creating increased demand (more jobs). In a *laissez-faire* economy, unemployment could only be a temporary phenomenon, and all was for the very best – and could only be harmed by "bureaucratic" (government) interference. The equivalent to *laissez faire* in international terms was Free Trade. From an economic point of view, the role of government was essentially to maintain Free Trade and make sure that the nation's currency remained stable, mainly through the Gold Standard.

In practice, complete *laissez faire* had never been allowed. Before all the old restrictions had been thrown off in the nineteenth century, new ones had been imposed – for example, factory acts that limited child labour and other forms of exploitation caused by unregulated competition. And by the early twentieth century foreign competition was hurting British industries badly enough to make some politicians advocate the replacement of Free Trade with a policy of protecting British manufactures in the home market by imposing duties on imports to make them more expensive.

Nevertheless, *laissez faire* remained the dominant economic philosophy down to the First World War of 1914–18. The war changed everything: during this life-and-death struggle the Government took control of British industry, and Free Trade and the Gold Standard were abandoned. When peace returned, some people argued that "war socialism" had proved highly successful, but most politicians and economists were eager to return to "normality", despite the fact that both the national and the international economies were much more fragile than they had been in 1914. Wartime controls were rapidly removed and protective duties gradually reduced. Finally, the return to the Gold Standard, carried out in 1925 by Winston Churchill as Chancellor of the Exchequer, completed the return to pre-war normality.

Yet it was already clear that orthodox economics failed to explain Britain's situation in the 1920s, with its rapid fluctuations in trade, its prolonged industrial disputes, and above all its distressed areas and high unemployment, which seemed to have become an inexplicably permanent feature of the industrial scene. Faith in the "automatic adjustments" offered by the Gold Standard and similar mechanisms was denounced in the early 1920s by the economist John Maynard Keynes, who wrote prophetically of the dangerous complacency shown by British politicians and financial interests:

I think they are immensely rash in their regardlessness, in their vague optimism and comfortable belief that nothing really serious ever happens. Nine times out of ten, nothing really serious does happen – merely a little distress to individuals or to groups. But we run a risk of the tenth time. (*The Economic Consequences of Mr Churchill*, 1925)

Laissez-faire theories did not work in the real world, Keynes asserted:

The world is *not* so governed from above that private and social interest always coincide. It is *not* so managed here below that in practice they coincide. It is *not* a correct deduction from the Principles of Economics that enlightened self-interest always operates in the public interest. Nor is it true that self-interest generally *is* enlightened; more often individuals acting separately to promote their own ends are too ignorant or too weak to attain even these. (*Essays in Persuasion*, 1931)

John Maynard Keynes was the son of a lecturer at Cambridge University, and after studying there he worked in the Civil Service before returning to his old college, King's, as a fellow. He was a man of wide interests, closely connected with the "Bloomsbury Group" of writers and artists, which included such famous figures as Virginia Woolf, Lytton Strachey and E.M. Forster. Later in life he would play an important role in theatrical developments and in the foundation of the Arts Council.

During the First World War, Keynes worked for the Treasury, which he represented at the subsequent Paris Peace Conference. He made his first impact on a wider public by resigning in disgust and publishing *The Economic Consequences of the Peace* (1919), which denounced the punitive treatment of Germany and in particular the belief that she could be made "to pay for the war" through reparations.

Back at King's, Keynes developed the ideas that were to make him the most influential economist of the twentieth century. He published them in epoch-making books such as *A Treatise on Money* (1930) and *The General Theory of Employment, Interest and Money* (1936). Much of the argument in these works is, of course, highly technical, and in this book there is only enough space to mention two Keynsian concepts of particular relevance to

FIRST AID TO INDUSTRY.

The Chancellor of the Exchequer. "IT DOESN'T SEEM TO GO SOMEHOW. THE SELF STARTER'S BROKE."
The Economic Expert. "DON'T KEEP ON SITTING THERE, MATE. OUT OUT AND GIVE 'ER A SWING."

[In a series of articles in *The Times* Mr J. M. Keynes has recommended the Government to adopt a policy of "wise spending" as a cure for our present ills.]

30 In this *Punch* cartoon, the economist John Maynard Keynes figures as the mechanic who could get the engine of British industry started again. However, the Government paid little heed to the "wise spending" recommended by Keynes.

31 A 1931 cartoon which expressed popular fears ▶ that money might lose its value, leaving barter as the only form of buying and selling.

PAYMENT IN KIND.

WHAT THE FALL FROM THE GOLD STANDARD MIGHT BRING US TO.

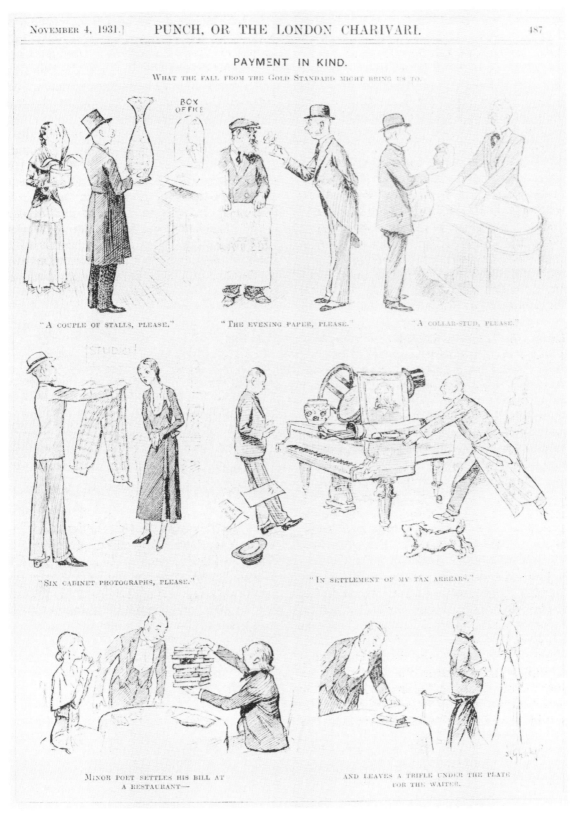

"A COUPLE OF STALLS, PLEASE."　　"THE EVENING PAPER, PLEASE."　　"A COLLAR-STUD, PLEASE."

"SIX CABINET PHOTOGRAPHS, PLEASE."　　"IN SETTLEMENT OF MY TAX ARREARS."

MINOR POET SETTLES HIS BILL AT
A RESTAURANT—　　AND LEAVES A TRIFLE UNDER THE PLATE
FOR THE WAITER.

the Depression: the concept of public works as a counter to unemployment, and the concept of the managed economy.

By "public works", Keynes meant government-funded (or government-subsidized) projects such as road- or house-building, which would provide more jobs. During the 1920s, and even more markedly during the Depression, unemployment caused a decline in the workers' purchasing power, which meant that fewer goods were produced and even fewer employees were needed. The result – still higher unemployment – meant yet another drop in purchasing power, production and employment; and so on, in a downward spiral. Apart from its social benefits, a programme of public works would put the process into reverse, creating a demand for, say, building materials and giving workers and their families extra purchasing power; the increased demand would be met by higher production, which would itself involve taking on more workers, whose purchasing power would lead to increased demand, more production and more jobs. In other words, a public works programme would benefit many times more people than the number to whom it gave immediate employment.

To the argument that the government could not afford large-scale projects, Keynes replied that it should borrow, although such "deficit spending" seemed outrageous to politicians who still believed that national finance was like housekeeping, a matter of balancing the budget at all costs. During the 1920s Keynes was closely associated with the Liberal Party, and Lloyd George, the Liberal leader, took up the policy of public spending to combat unemployment as part of his 1929 election manifesto. But the subsequent Labour Government remained orthodox in outlook, and in July 1931 a committee of inquiry, the May Committee, presented a wildly exaggerated account of British difficulties and recommended dole-cutting and other ruthless economies. Keynes trenchantly dismissed the Committee's findings as "the most foolish document I ever had the misfortune to read",

but after the fall of Labour and the formation of the National Government, stringent economies were introduced which have already been described. To "save the pound", the dole was cut and the Means Test introduced. Yet, within weeks Britain had been forced off the Gold Standard, and within months Free Trade had been abandoned. The "economies", however, remained.

Over the years, Keynes developed a wider programme. He asserted that governments should not leave the economy to the play of market forces but should intervene to manage it. By public works, by using the budget to stimulate or discourage business activity, by Bank of England operations on the Stock Exchange, and in various other ways, the government should take responsibility for creating a prosperous society in which there was full employment. Keynes himself wrote in 1939 that

The question is whether we are prepared to move out of the nineteenth century *laissez faire* state into an era of liberal socialism, by which I mean a system where we can act as an organized community for common purposes and to promote social and economic justice whilst respecting and protecting the individual. (From an article in the *New Statesman*, 1939)

Ironically, by the time these words were written the public spending solution had begun to be adopted in one of its least palatable forms: rearmament, occasioned by the threat from Hitler's Germany. Earlier in the 1930s Keynes had been frequently consulted by British governments, and his influence made itself felt remarkably quickly – but, given the slow pace of government and civil service ruminations, not quickly enough to make a substantial impact on the Depression. The triumph of the "Keynsian revolution" occurred in 1944, when the White Paper on Employment Policy embraced his ideas, which largely determined the way in which the British economy was run for the following 35 years.

Joseph Goebbels (1897-1945)

Even before the Depression, Germans had experienced a series of painful and bewildering changes in their political and social lives. After suffering near-starvation because of the Allied blockade, they had seen their country go down to defeat in November 1918. Their emperor, Kaiser Wilhelm II, had abdicated, and the monarchy had been replaced by the democratic Weimar Republic. Political, military and financial penalties were imposed on the new republic by the victorious Allies, and in 1923, when Germany experienced difficulties in keeping up her reparations payments, French troops occupied the Ruhr. German attempts at passive resistance led to yet another catastrophe – a massive and rapid inflation which wiped out most people's life savings, impoverishing and embittering a large section of the German middle class. With such a background of fearful shocks only a few years before, the Depression would have a more shattering effect on Germany than on any other country.

In the early years of Weimar there were many active nationalist and right-wing groups, bitterly hostile to the new democratic republic. One of these was the National Socialist, or Nazi, Party, led by Adolf Hitler, who was to rise to power at the height of the Depression. Hitler blamed Germany's troubles on the Jews, the Communists and the "November criminals" – the democratic politicians who had (supposedly) betrayed Germany's (supposedly) still-undefeated army by capitulating at Versailles. Hitler promised that when he took power he would scrap democracy in favour of a one-party state based on the "leader-principle", and that he would "purify" the German race, tear up the Versailles treaties and make Germany strong again.

The crisis of 1923 seemed like a golden opportunity to carry out these plans. But when Hitler tried to seize power in the south German state of Bavaria, the Putsch (revolt) in Munich was a fiasco and Hitler himself ended up in prison. Even worse (from a Nazi point of view) was the impressive recovery made by the Weimar Republic. Between 1924 and 1929 Germany enjoyed a reasonable prosperity, though it was dangerously dependent on American loans that discharged reparations payments and financed the re-equipment of German industry. Unemployment had remained a problem, but by 1928 it was down to 650,000. The Nazi Party, which could only thrive on discontent, secured less than a million votes in the 1928 general election, sending a mere 12 members to the Reichstag.

32 Dr Goebbels, chief propagandist for Adolf Hitler and the Nazi Party, in a characteristic speech-making pose.

The principal Nazi leaders during and for some time after the Putsch were Hitler and Hermann Göring, a tough ex-fighter ace with useful political and social contacts. During the 1920s a third figure emerged: the brilliant, unscrupulous propagandist Dr Joseph Goebbels. Unlike Hitler and Göring, Goebbels was small, lame (he was rejected for military service during the First World War), and very much an intellectual; he had studied at several universities and had been awarded a PhD – the doctorate of philosophy that entitled him to be called "Dr Goebbels". To some extent he was a victim of Germany's post-war difficulties, failing to find the sort of job which his qualifications might have led him to expect; with rather more justice, publishers turned down his novel *Michael* and newspapers rejected his journalistic efforts. Then, in 1924, he joined the Nazis and came into prominence as the secretary of the party's North German leader, Gregor Strasser.

Among other things, the Nazi Party programme took a strong anti-capitalist stance. Strasser and Goebbels belonged to the radical wing of the party, which emphasized its revolutionary and socialist character in opposition to Hitler, who was interested in social and economic issues only in so far as they could be exploited for political advantage. Impressed by the ease with which a detachment of armed police had put down the Munich Putsch, Hitler was also convinced that the Nazis could only make their revolution *after* they had somehow gained power by legal means. In 1926, when the tensions between Strasser and Hitler came close to breaking point, Goebbels is said to have demanded the expulsion of "the petty bourgeois Adolf Hitler" from the party.

A few weeks later, Goebbels had changed his mind. Some writers have suggested that he was impressed by the more affluent lifestyle of Hitler and the Bavarian party chiefs, but there seems no doubt about the sincerity of his devotion to Hitler. From this time onwards, Goebbels used all his considerable gifts to create a cult of Hitler which helped to make the Führer unchallengeable within the party and a legendary, god-like figure outside it.

The first great step in Goebbels' own career as a master propagandist was taken in the autumn of 1926, when Hitler put him in charge of the party in the German capital, Berlin. There, through speeches, articles in the newspaper he founded, *Der Angrieff* ("The Attack"), and a series of ingenious stunts, provocations and outrages (committed by the party's brown-shirted private army, the SA), Goebbels made the Nazi Party known and felt. Following Hitler's own theories, he paid little attention to reasoned argument, but, as he himself confessed, appealed to people's "most primitive instincts". Uniforms, banners, chanting masses, parades and torchlight processions: he aimed to create an image of Nazism as driven by a ruthless, superhuman will, believing that the masses worshipped strength above all things. As for truth, that was as irrelevant as reason: "Propaganda has absolutely nothing to do with truth!"

Yet for all the Nazis' skill as propagandists they made little progress until the Depression hit Germany; though people did resent the Versailles Treaty, did harbour many grievances, and did possess many of the prejudices exploited by the Nazis, these feelings only became dominant when the economic foundations of their lives seemed to be collapsing. Goebbels welcomed the crisis; as early as 1926, he had written:

We shall achieve everything if we set hunger, despair and sacrifice on the march for our goals.

In the face of economic disaster, the climate of opinion did, in fact, change rapidly. In September 1930, when there were already three million unemployed, the Nazis registered a huge success, increasing their seats in the Reichstag from 12 to 107 and becoming the second largest party. As well as an economic crisis, there was now a political stalemate: no party or coalition could obtain a majority in the Reichstag, and a series of chancellors (German prime ministers) ruled through the special powers of the aged President, Paul von Hindenburg – a situation in which backstairs intrigues flourished, and one that Hitler could hope to exploit.

The economic situation grew steadily worse as American loans dried up, the failure of the Viennese Kreditanstalt rocked Central Europe, the big Darmstädter und National bank closed its doors, bankruptcies multiplied, and the number of unemployed reached six million in early 1932. In a series of local and presidential elections the Nazi vote continued to increase, until, in the general election of July 1932, the party won 230 of the 608 seats. Though still far short of an overall majority, it was now easily the largest political party in Germany. For Goebbels, these were years of frenzied activity:

Once more eternally on the move. Work has to be done standing, walking, driving, flying. The most urgent conferences are held on the stairs, in the hall, at the door, or on the way to the station . . . . The audience generally has no idea of what the speaker has already gone through during the day before he makes his speech in the evening.

Some of his cleverest slogans date from this period, for example "Hitler Over Germany", which highlighted the Führer's unusual tactic of making flights all over the country to speak at mass meetings, while also delivering a straightforward political message.

It was no coincidence that the rise of Nazism and the onset of the Depression occurred simultaneously. The desperate situation encouraged people to vote for "strong" solutions, and the diametrically opposite party of radical change, the Communist Party, also made considerable progress. The Communists were dangerous competition for the working-class vote, though they never possessed the Nazis' broader appeal. But Hitler and Goebbels found it increasingly difficult to maintain this appeal, which was based on sleight of hand: while being subsidized by big business, they assured the workers and lower middle class that they would smash the big trusts and combines. By late 1932 there were signs that some Nazi voters were losing patience and going over to the Communists; and when the Communists staged a transport strike, the Nazis felt they must prove their radicalism by joining in, seriously alarming their big business connections. At a new general election in November 1932, the Party met its first setback, losing two million votes and being reduced to 196 seats.

The Nazis may well have passed their peak, but within a few weeks the intriguers around Hindenburg had fallen out, and Hitler got his chance at last. On 30 January 1933 he became German Chancellor at the head of a coalition government. His conservative colleagues believed they had "tamed" him; but he proved them wrong in a matter of months, using the power of the state to eliminate all opposition and become the all-powerful Führer of the Third Reich.

33 This Nazi poster presents all workers in the Third Reich as comrades. In reality, German workers lost most of their rights under Hitler, but after the high unemployment of the Depression years they were glad to have jobs at all.

Hitler's tyranny, his foreign policy successes and his plunge into World War are well known and need not be described here – unlike his handling of the Depression, which was still at its height when he took power. Economically, the Nazis' radicalism was soon seen to be a sham. Faithful to the leader-principle, Hitler left the employers in charge of their business and factories, tied employees to their places of work, and outlawed strikes. But he also transformed the economy and wiped out unemployment. Although he was helped by an improvement in the international economic situation, the main credit belongs to his "Keynsian" public spending programme. To some extent this was an accidental success, since the spending was mainly on the military preparations that Hitler considered essential for his foreign policy – rearmament, including the expansion and mechanization of the armed forces (restricted by Versailles), plus major public works such as a great system of motorways (autobahns) to facilitate their mobility. However undesirable the intention behind it, the policy worked. And, as William L. Shirer noted, it did a good deal to reconcile the German worker to his lot:

. . . the greatest cause of his acceptance of his role in Nazi Germany was, without any doubt at all, that he had a job again and the assurance that he would keep it. (*The Rise and Fall of the Third Reich*)

Goebbels received his reward in 1933, becoming Minister of National Enlightenment and Propaganda. Having announced that "the Government intends no longer to leave the people to their own devices", he placed all the media under rigid control, made bonfires of the writings of "enemies" from Karl Marx to Albert Einstein, and made certain that only the Nazi voice was heard throughout Germany until his death in the ruins of the Third Reich.

34 The opening of the first *Autobahn*, or motorway – the beginning of a spectacular road-building programme that helped to pull Germany out of the Depression.

Franklin D. Roosevelt (1882-1945)

When Americans went to the polls to elect a new president in November 1932, the Depression had been in full swing for over three years. During that time, President Herbert Hoover had become discredited by his frequent and futile predictions that prosperity was just around the corner, so no one was surprised when he lost the election to the Democratic Party's candidate, Franklin Delano Roosevelt. Hoover had not been completely inactive; he had set up a Reconstruction Finance Corporation to help businesses in difficulties, and had reacted sensibly to the international spread of the Depression by suspending the collection of debts owed to the United States by European countries. But he had done nothing to help the millions of Americans thrown out of work or impoverished by the economic blizzard. These suffering millions wanted much more vigorous action, and turned to Roosevelt, who had told his fellow Democrats: "I pledge you, I pledge myself, to a new deal for the American people." The policies adopted by Roosevelt's administration between 1933 and 1940 have gone down in history as "the New Deal".

At first sight, Roosevelt seemed an unlikely popular saviour-figure. He was (in American terms) an aristocrat, coming from an old and wealthy New York family of Dutch extraction. His public image was also aristocratic – that of a man who wore old-fashioned pince-nez (spectacles without earpieces) and flourished a cigarette-holder. He had advanced steadily and shrewdly within the Democratic Party, becoming an increasingly conspicuous public figure despite an attack of polio in 1921 which left him severely disabled. As governor of New York (1928-32) he had shown his willingness to use the resources at his disposal to help the unemployed; and as president he introduced a programme of state intervention on a massive scale.

This was an extraordinary departure in the America of 1933. It entailed the rejection of *laissez-faire* economic doctrine; but, even more radically, it embodied a new view of what an American president's administration could or should accomplish. A British prime minister, backed by a majority of MPs in the House of Commons, can pass more or less any laws, or take almost any action, that he or she believes to be useful. But in the United States a written constitution lays down what kinds of laws the Congress may pass, and what sort of actions the administration may undertake. The Supreme Court exists to determine whether or not a measure is constitutional – that is, not whether the measure seems a good or a bad one, but whether it is within the powers of (say) the President to act in the matter at all. In practice, however, constitutions – and also most laws – can be "reinterpreted" to meet new situations, if the judges are sympathetic to change. The men who framed the American Constitution had intended to protect the sovereignty of the individual states in the Union, leaving only a few functions necessary for the common good to Congress and the federal government (the US government at Washington D.C., headed by the president). But over the years, as society grew more complex, the federal government took on many more responsibilities and exercised wider powers than the "Founding Fathers" had intended; and the meanings read into the Constitution changed accordingly. Even so, the New Deal extended federal action to a quite unprecedented extent, and it is necessary to appreciate this in order to understand its enormous impact – and its unpopularity in conservative quarters.

When Roosevelt took office in March 1933, the United States was in the throes of a new crisis, caused by an epidemic of bank failures. Such epidemics were in large measure the result of lack of confidence felt in America's financial institutions: if one bank failed, frightened depositors elsewhere started making withdrawals from *their* banks, and as each "run on the bank" caused new closures, confidence declined further, creating yet another downward spiral of new panics and new closures. In his inaugural speech, Roosevelt pointed to confidence as a key factor in the situation:

the only thing we have to fear is fear itself – nameless, unreasoning, unjustified terror which paralyses needed efforts to convert retreat into advance.

Having declared a national bank holiday to "freeze" the situation, the President rushed through Congress an Act that greatly increased government control over the banks, eliminated some of the weakest, and in effect issued a state guarantee of the rest so that depositors' fears were allayed. Later, using the Reconstruction Finance Corporation set up by Hoover, the Government acquired enough shares in the major banks to direct investment and expansion into the areas it believed to be of the greatest national benefit. American stock exchanges were also brought under control, and their modes of operation tightened up. To revive hope and confidence – and also, of course, to maintain his own popularity – Roosevelt became a familiar presence in most American homes, using the relatively new medium of radio to give regular "fireside chats" that kept ordinary people in touch with the State of the Nation. (He also improved American spirits in another sense, by repealing the Volstead Act of 1919 which imposed "Prohibition" on the entire United States. Until 1933 Americans were not allowed to manufacture or consume alcoholic drinks – the result being that they drank more than ever, illicitly, at "speakeasies" supplied by gangsters and tolerated by corrupt officials.)

"The Hundred Days" – the first three months of Roosevelt's administration – became famous for the spate of legislation pushed through Congress on the initiative of the New Dealers. In fact, most of the essential ideas and institutions of the New Deal were foreshadowed in this period, though they were

35 Franklin Delano Roosevelt broadcasting the first of his "fireside chats" in December 1933.

36 A cartoon view of the New Deal: ex-President ▶ Hoover leaves the White House, while Roosevelt puts out the garbage – Hoover's promises and the policies of the Republican Party (nicknamed the G.O.P. – Grand Old Party).

often consolidated or reshaped in later years. There were two interlinked tasks to be tackled: the relief of suffering and the creation of new jobs. Unlike Britain and Germany, the United States had no social security scheme run by the government; the unemployed and needy were dependent on very sparse local or individual initiatives which were generally no more than charitable hand-outs. The Federal Relief Emergency Act provided an initial $500 million for immediate distribution, and a later Social Security Act laid the basis of a nationwide welfare scheme to which workers contributed and from which they drew benefits, as of right, when they were unemployed. The most pressing problem for American farmers and their families, who accounted for a quarter of the population, was to keep up their mortgage repayments on pain of losing their land. Here the Farm Credit Act fended off the worst by acting as the farmer's guarantor. It was never claimed that, in the absence of a national scheme and existing national agencies, these measures could do more than alleviate hardship, but they far surpassed anything that previous administrations had attempted.

In his inaugural speech, Roosevelt made a firm commitment to creating jobs through public works projects. Putting people to work, he said,

can be accomplished in part by direct recruiting by the government itself, treating the task as we would treat the emergency of a war, but at the same time, through this employment,

accomplishing greatly needed projects to stimulate and reorganize the use of our national resources.

The most famous example of this was the Tennessee Valley Authority (TVA), the first public electricity authority in the USA. Starting with federally owned dams in the Tennessee Valley, the authority undertook a campaign of expansion that created jobs, promoted soil conservation and brought electricity to thousands of poor homes. There were many other "alphabetical" federal agencies, such as the PWA (Public Works Administration), which undertook the

PHIA RECORD, FRIDAY, MARCH 3, 1933

FINIS.   —By Jerry Doyle

building of highways, bridges and similar projects; the WPA (Works Progress Administration), which employed thousands of writers and artists; and the CCC (Civilian Conservation Corps), which provided government-enrolled labour, in the form of a quarter-million-strong force of young unemployed men, to tackle large-scale public works. Altogether, billions of dollars were spent, and something like six million new jobs were created.

Much of the New Deal was improvised, and its overlapping agencies and sometimes fanciful projects were sharply criticized. All the same, Americans recognized Roosevelt's achievement, and he was re-elected with ease in 1936. However, conservatives in his own party, as well as Republicans, were becoming increasingly incensed at what they saw as the President's radicalism. The federal government had taken wide powers to direct American industry, often to the advantage of businessmen, who were allowed to form trusts and combines in a way that had previously been illegal. (Like "rationalization" in Britain, this was intended to strengthen and modernize industry.) But other aspects of federal activities – the promotion of trade unionism, higher wages and improved working conditions – were resented by most industrialists. They, along with other enemies of the administration, rejoiced when the Supreme Court stepped in and condemned as unconstitutional large parts of the New Deal, including some of its most progressive legislation on working conditions.

As a result, Roosevelt's second term of office was disfigured by bitter quarrels with the Supreme Court and increasing difficulties with Congress which consumed time and energy. With the Depression still far from overcome, the New Dealers' energies seemed to be flagging; and then, in 1937, the economy plunged again. This was at least partly the result of an "anti-inflationary" budget. Despite his bold projects, Roosevelt had never freed himself from orthodox economic ideas, as he had shown during the Hundred Days – by slashing civil servants' salaries as a sop to

THE SOWER.

37 The image of Roosevelt as America's saviour.

"sound" finance. Now he was persuaded that it was time to cut public spending and produce a properly balanced budget – with disastrous results: unemployment rose by two million before the end of the year. As in Britain, the Depression was not to be finally overcome until rearmament and war provided work and incentives for all.

Its uneven performance makes it difficult to assess the New Deal. Even now, some writers dismiss it as a sort of confidence trick or mass illusion which brought no solid benefits. But although no one can say how well (or badly) an alternative policy would have worked, Roosevelt's successes do seem impressive when it is remembered that the American economy seemed on the point of total collapse when he took over, and that he had to create a programme of effective state action almost from scratch. In the last analysis, the American people showed their approval in the most direct fashion in 1940, sending Franklin D. Roosevelt to the White House for a third term, during which he became their leader in war as well as in peace.

Depression Culture

Frank Capra (1897-   )

The cinema was the great popular art of the early twentieth century, appealing to millions of people who had never been reached by traditional arts such as the theatre and literature. The changeover from silent films to "talkies", which occurred during the late 1920s, further increased the appeal of the cinema. "The pictures" were the cheapest form of entertainment, yet they were produced with high skill and featured world-famous stars. In style and spectacle they easily

38 The movies first cast their spell on the public during the "silent" era. Rudolph Valentino, "the Great Lover", was idolized by millions.

surpassed alternatives such as the music-hall and the circus. The hard-up hero of Walter Greenwood's *Love on the Dole* could always look forward to the weekend, when

There'd be the picture queue – always fun there – the fourpenny seats; perhaps a penn'orth of chipped potatoes each, wrapped in a piece of newspaper: wouldn't be Saturday night lacking these.

Their mass appeal meant that most films were escapist. In the 1920s the Soviet cinema produced a number of great films inspired by the ideals of the 1917 Revolution, and the cinema was sometimes treated as a "serious" art in Germany and other European countries. But the entire western world was dominated by Hollywood. In the silent era, when they were not laughing at the antics of Charlie Chaplin's little tramp, audiences were thrilling to the adventures of Douglas Fairbanks as Don Juan or the Thief of Baghdad, and the exotic love-making of Rudolf Valentino in his roles as the Sheik or the doomed matador in *Blood and Sand*.

The Depression did not make American films more topically political or social in outlook. A few famous documentaries, such as *The Plow That Broke the Plains*, were sponsored by the Roosevelt administration in an effort to explain the New Deal to the American people. Their circulation was restricted, however, since most cinemas (like most newspapers and radio corporations) were in the hands of people hostile to Roosevelt. The handful of more radical ventures of course faced even greater difficulties.

With a few exceptions, Hollywood continued to be a "dream factory". But, perhaps because of the Depression, there were many more films featuring modern settings and characters with whom ordinary Americans could identify, even though the plots usually remained in the realms of fantasy. The most down-to-earth were the gangster movies, which came into their own around 1930; the main characters were poor boys who made good (through being bad) until the final reel, when morality and the censor insisted that they must come to a sticky end. Musical films were also given the common touch. A favourite plot concerned the tribulations of "putting on a show", since the characters were "ordinary", likeable actors, dancers and composers, often supposedly down on their luck; at the same time, the "show" they eventually managed to stage provided an excuse for lavish and spectacular musical numbers. In *Gold Diggers of 1933* the "show" is actually a musical about the Depression, and the film ends with a long on-stage set-piece, "My Forgotten Man", complete with a chorus of down-and-outs in a soup-kitchen queue!

Hollywood "screwball" comedies appealed directly to the longing for wealth and security – and all the more effectively for their apparently realistic and up-to-date settings. Typically, poor boy (girl) meets rich girl (boy) and, after appropriate complications, marries her (him). Ordinary people – including the audience – are flattered by a harmless kind of social criticism: the rich girl (boy) is often portrayed as spoiled or irresponsible, and has to be brought to her (his) senses by the poor boy (girl). In general, the rich tend to be shown as joyless prisoners of their status; their money insulates them from the real world, and it is the poor who are wise – and who know how to have fun.

One outstanding exponent of this kind of film was the director Frank Capra. In Capra's *It Happened One Night* (1934), the newspaper reporter Peter Warne (Clark Gable) aids the runaway heiress Ellie Andrews (Claudette Colbert), who is ignorant and helpless without her money. Before the inevitable romantic ending she has learned a lot – even the art of dunking a doughnut in coffee without spoiling it. Capra's earlier *Platinum Blonde* (1931) is a variation on the same theme: a reporter marries a rich girl, but cannot bear her social set and returns to his own kind. Here, too, it is the life of ordinary people that is seen as somehow more "real" than that of the rich.

The cult of the common man in America was "good box-office", and very much in tune with the mood of the times. But there is no doubt that Capra, at least, had a genuine belief

39 Shooting one of the famous Greyhound bus scenes of *It Happened One Night*. Capra (left, hands in the pockets of his long raincoat) is directing Clark Gable (centre, holding a newspaper).

in the essential goodness of Americans, and this gives his work much of its special quality. *It Happened One Night* vividly conveys a sense of Americans on the move, travelling in long-distance buses and staying overnight in cheap motels – as huge numbers of Americans, uprooted by the Depression, were in fact doing. One of the most effective scenes occurs at night on the bus, when the passengers and driver give a rendition of "That Daring Young Man on the Flying Trapeze"; though inserted between episodes of an amusing but absurd plot, this seems like a spontaneous outburst of fellow-feeling rather than a musical routine.

Capra's remedies for the Depression are goodwill and mutual helpfulness. *American Madness* (1931), for example, was (in Capra's own words)

a story about a banker who trusted the people. He loaned the money more on character than he did on collateral [security], much to the disgust of his board of directors and other bankers all around. Finally he got into a jam . . . and there was a run on the bank. But he was saved by the same people that he trusted, who came to his help in whatever way they could, and that made everything okay for him.

One of Capra's most famous films, *Mr Deeds Goes to Town* (1936), implicitly recommends a more specific measure. Longfellow Deeds, a small-town American,

▲

40 A still from *Mr Deeds Goes to Town*: Mr Deeds (Gary Cooper, right) takes an unemployed man out to dinner at a grand restaurant.

41 A real-life Mr Deeds. At the Ritz Hotel Restaurant, a Mr Spreckley gives a lunch for six men who had been out of work for more than three years. A careful comparison between the real and the fictitious scenes will yield some interesting conclusions.

▼

unexpectedly inherits $20 million. Despite his apparent simplicity he fends off the smart-talking New Yorkers who try to make him part with his money; but he is betrayed by a woman friend – actually a reporter – who ridicules his naively "eccentric" behaviour in the press. When Mr Deeds proposes to help victims of the Depression by setting them up as small farmers, a crooked lawyer exploits Deeds' reputation to cast doubt on his sanity, and Deeds is forced to fight for his freedom as well as his fortune.

Capra continued to make notable films in the 1930s and 1940s, including *Mr Smith Goes to Washington* (1939) and *Meet John Doe* (1941). But after *It's A Wonderful Life* (1946), the climate of feeling in the United States was less sympathetic to his optimistic "populist" outlook, and his career gradually petered out.

Bertolt Brecht (1898-1956)

During its brief, turbulent history, the Weimar Republic was a major centre of the modern arts. At the Bauhaus, a college based at Weimar (1919-25) and later at Dessau (1925-33), some of the leading European artists and architects worked to bring about a revolution in industrial design. Avant-garde ("advanced") literature and music flourished in Germany, though (as elsewhere) many people were scandalized by the new techniques employed and by the content, which was often politically radical or socially unconventional. This was also true of films and plays, in which both the example and the outlook of the great Soviet film-makers proved influential. In the theatre, a number of writers and directors broke with the conventions of realistic staging and dialogue, usually in order to put over a political message as forcefully as possible. Although not the first, the dramatist Bertolt Brecht was undoubtedly the greatest of these theatrical innovators.

Brecht was a South German, born and brought up in the Bavarian city of Augsburg. He became a medical student at Munich University, but his studies were interrupted in 1916, when he was drafted into the army as a medical orderly. Working in a military hospital, he witnessed at first hand the horrible effects of trench warfare. With anger and disgust he "saw how they patched up people in order to ship them back to the front as soon as possible". In a satirical poem by Brecht, "Legend of the Dead Soldier" (1918), the need for more and more cannon-fodder leads to the digging up of a soldier's corpse, which is promptly examined and declared fit for active service.

Though already a rebel and anti-militarist, Brecht made an increasingly successful career as a playwright during the 1920s. In 1928 he became famous with *The Threepenny Opera*, which is set in the thieves' dens and brothels of an imaginary Victorian London; the music by Kurt Weill (1900-50) ranges from the abrasive to the mock-sentimental, in a jazz-influenced idiom that exactly matched the mood and style of Brecht's lyrics.

Although the world of *The Threepenny Opera* is shown as deeply corrupt, no obviously political moral is drawn at the end of the work. Nevertheless, Brecht's disillusion with the established order had been strengthened by Germany's post-war troubles, and by the late 1920s he had become committed to communism, though he never formally joined the Communist Party. His sympathies were already fairly clear in his plays and poems, but the onset of the Depression and the Nazi menace encouraged him to make increasingly direct political statements. When arrangements were made to film *The Threepenny Opera* he wrote a script in

42 The German playwright Bertolt Brecht.

which the link between crime and capitalism was made clear: Macheath, the robber hero, ends up as the admired president of a bank. (This version was never used; Brecht sued the producers but failed to prevent the filming of a different script.) The extremes of wealth and poverty were glaringly obvious in Berlin, where Brecht had lived since 1924. The German capital is the "Mahagonny" of *The Rise and Fall of the City of Mahagonny* (1930), portrayed as a lawless frontier town where most crimes are condoned, but one – lack of money – merits the death penalty.

Brecht was also co-author of the script for a film, *Kuhle Wampe* (1932), set in a squalid shanty town on the outskirts of Berlin. Its grim story includes the suicide of an unemployed youth, and only at the end is there a glimpse of hope, in the sense of human solidarity generated by a Communist sports rally. When the censor saw the film he decided to ban it: an individual suicide was a permissible tragic subject, he told Brecht and his colleagues, but *Kuhle Wampe* went beyond that in showing the youth as a symbolic figure, representing a generation that was being destroyed – and that was *not* permissible. Amazingly, Brecht managed to convince the censor that he was wrong, and that the suicide was simply the story of a single unlucky individual. Brecht was, of course, lying. As he later wrote,

43 A scene from the film of Brecht's *The Threepenny Opera.*

Leaving the building we did not conceal our high opinion of the censor. He had penetrated the essence of our artistic intentions with far greater sagacity than our most benevolent critics.

By this time, Brecht had developed a new theory of the drama which fitted in with his own practice and his political beliefs. Brechtian theatre is "epic", as opposed to the conventional "dramatic" theatre, which more or less directly imitates real life. Brecht's objection to the "dramatic" play was that the spectator became so involved in it that he forgot it was a play. He identified with the characters and became immersed in the action, which – if the play was "well made" – ran a seemingly inevitable course. At the end of it, he was emotionally drained, but had learned nothing. As Brecht puts it,

The spectator of the *dramatic* theatre says: 'Yes, I have felt the same. – I am just like this. – This is only natural. – It will always be like this. This human being's suffering moved me, because there is no way out for him. This is great art: it bears the mark of the inevitable.'

Brecht wanted a different kind of theatre: one that would move people, but would also make them think carefully about the stage action and draw conclusions from it about the real world. Unlike the ordinary theatre-goer, who is "swept away", the Brechtian spectator should watch in a critical spirit, much as the sports fan does, remaining able to comment and think of improvements at even the most exciting moments. The most unusual features of the Brechtian play are designed to interrupt the action so that the spectators will not be swept away, but will remain aware that it *is* a play; hence the actors may carry about notices making political points, a narrator may intervene to explain or criticize a situation, or an actor may stop in mid-speech and address the audience. According to Brecht himself,

The spectator of the *epic* theatre says: 'I should never have thought so. – That isn't the way to do it. This is most surprising, hardly credible. – This will have to stop. – This human being's suffering

moves me because there was a way out for him. This is great art: nothing here seems inevitable.'

In other words, the spectator finds that the world ought to be, and can be, changed. In *St Joan of the Stockyards*, the way to change it is made explicit. This play was suggested by Brecht's investigations of the soup-kitchens run by the Salvation Army in Berlin, and his heroine is first seen as a member of a fictitious Salvation-Army-style organization; but she dies proclaiming the necessity of using revolutionary violence to change the social system.

By 1932, when *St Joan of the Stockyards* was ready for performance, the political climate was such that no German theatre would accept it. Soon Adolf Hitler had become Chancellor of Germany, and less than a month later, on 27 February 1933, the Reichstag fire gave the Nazis an excuse for mass arrests of Communists. Brecht, high on the Nazis' lists, left Germany the very next day. He was to spend 15 years in exile, a dramatist without an audience, during which time he wrote some of his most famous plays.

44 May 1933: Stormtroopers and students carrying "un-German" literature to the bonfire. By this time Brecht had already fled from Germany. His writings, and those of many other famous authors, were burned and banned in the Third Reich.

Ben Shahn (1897-1969)

There were many artists and architects among the people who fell on hard times during the Depression. Painters and sculptors produce relatively expensive items and can only thrive if affluent individuals or organizations are willing to buy their works. Architects are even more dependent, since they cannot begin to build until someone has commissioned them and provided the necessary land, materials and labour. But the Crash and the Depression hit many wealthy individuals and businesses, and made the rest cautious about what they did with their money. Since art has generally been seen as a luxury that it is relatively easy to do without, patrons and commissions were scarce in the 1930s.

This was the situation facing the American painter Ben Shahn at the point in his career when he was beginning to work out his own distinctive style. From the age of 13 he had drudged in a lithographer's works, painstakingly financing his attendance at art college, study trips abroad, and his work as a painter. He made his breakthrough as an artist with a series of 23 paintings, "The Passion of Sacco and Vanzetti", based on a notorious miscarriage of American justice in the 1920s; Nicola Sacco and Bartolomeo Vanzetti, two poor Italian-born anarchists, were accused of a bank robbery, convicted on ludicrously inadequate evidence, and executed in 1927.

45 Ben Shahn's mural in commemoration of the Italian-born anarchists Sacco and Vanzetti, unjustly convicted of murder and executed in the USA.

During a period when many painters were producing fantastic, decorative or abstract works, and insisting that art was essentially independent of the real world, it had taken Shahn some time to realize that he felt differently.

'Here am I,' I said to myself, 'thirty-two years old, the son of a carpenter. I like stories and people. The French school is not for me.'

And his involvement with events and issues in the real world provided the key to his future work:

'Then I got to thinking about the Sacco-Vanzetti case . . . . Ever since I could remember I'd wished that I'd been lucky enough to be alive at a great time – when something big was going on, like the Crucifixion. And suddenly I realized I was. Here I was living through another crucifixion. Here was something to paint!'

Although the exhibition of Shahn's Sacco-Vanzetti paintings was a success, the Depression made the future look bleak – especially for an artist committed to left-wing and libertarian causes which many Americans regarded as "subversive". But for Shahn, as for so many Americans, the New Deal made a great difference. Through a number of schemes, the best known being the Federal Art Project (WPA), the government gave employment to as many as 5000 American artists, spending $19 million on their salaries and work. Some 1300 murals (large-scale wall paintings) were commissioned for public institutions, and no less than 48,000 oil paintings and watercolours. Various handicraft projects were launched, and artists and photographers, like writers, were sent to record and report on every aspect of American life. Inevitably, some of the schemes financed by the federal government were questionable, and critics accused WPA artists of sponging or "boondoggling" (carrying out useless tasks). But it can hardly be doubted that New Deal agencies kept the arts alive in the United States during the 1930s.

For Shahn, as for thousands of others, the government was the only employer of significance from 1933 until the Second World War. His activities give some idea of the scope of the federal schemes. He painted a set of panels on the subject of Prohibition for the Central Park Casino in New York. He made preliminary sketches for murals on the subject of penal reform, intended for the walls of a run-down New York penitentiary that was being improved – but the sketches were rejected by the traditionalist Municipal Art Commission. As Senior Liaison Officer of the Farm Security Administration (1935-8), he travelled the South and Middle West, making a photographic survey that involved taking 6000 pictures. He created a large mural for the community centre of Jersey Homesteads (now Roosevelt, New Jersey), a New Deal housing development for unemployed members of the International Ladies Garment Workers' Union and their families. Shahn felt at home at Jersey Homesteads and stayed on as a resident after his work there was finished. Typical of

◄ **46** Shahn's mural for the Jersey Homesteads community centre. It depicts the history of American garment workers, beginning with their experience as immigrants in the decades before the First World War. But Shahn also makes what was then a topical point, putting in the figure of the famous physicist Albert Einstein, a much more recent exile from Nazi Germany.

much of Shahn's large-scale work in the 1930s, the mural tells the story of the garment workers from immigration, through bitter struggle, to hard-won improvements in their legal rights and conditions. But, though dealing with the real world, the mural is not realistic in the photographic sense; the immigrants are shown as headed by the physicist Albert Einstein – a refugee from Nazi Germany – and coffins holding the

bodies of Sacco and Vanzetti are present as a warning against similar kinds of prejudice and persecution in the United States. In 1938-9 Shahn and his wife were commissioned to paint 13 panels for the Bronx Post Office, for which they chose the theme of work and workers in various parts of the USA. And in 1940-2 they produced a mural history of social security for the Social Security Building in Washington, D.C.

Since Shahn also executed a large number of easel paintings, his productivity as a federal employee was impressive. Though, like many others, he became disillusioned with the Communist Party, he remained a radical figure and vigorous champion of Roosevelt. Shahn continued to work in government service during the Second World War, designing a number of effective posters. With the coming of the affluent post-war period he was already known as one of America's outstanding painters, and was able to make a successful career in conventional fashion as an independent artist. For Shahn, the experience of living through the Depression was above all the experience of Roosevelt's New Deal.

John Steinbeck (1902-68)

The most famous novel about the Depression is John Steinbeck's *The Grapes of Wrath* (1940), which reads as though written in a white heat of anger. Steinbeck himself was born and brought up in the rich and fertile state of California. He came from a secure background, and although he identified strongly with ordinary people – working in the fields for a time and doing other manual jobs –

he quickly began to make his mark as a writer. Some of his works, for example *Tortilla Flat* (1935), were richly comic celebrations of life among the drop-outs of California's Salinas Valley. But Steinbeck's strong feelings about social injustice were already clear in an early novel such as *In Dubious Battle* (1936), which centres on a fruit-pickers' strike. He had seen for himself the plight of migrant workers who

47 The American novelist John Steinbeck.

Farmers had known hard times since the end of the First World War, when they and their families still accounted for a quarter of the American population. The most serious problems were caused by overproduction – the sheer abundance of produce which poured on to the market, keeping prices too low to provide the farmers with a decent standard of living. The Depression made matters even worse, since many people were too poor even to afford food at "give-away" prices; at times, farmers found it not worth the effort and expense to take their produce to market. The New Deal did something to alleviate the situation, though one of the most widely publicized measures was a counsel of despair: farmers were actually paid to burn their own crops and slaughter millions of piglets in order to combat overproduction. Although control of production was later organized more rationally, America's agricultural problems were largely solved by a longer-term, more painful process of adjustment that extended throughout the 1920s and 1930s. Willingly or otherwise, millions of Americans abandoned the land, and a mechanized farming industry eventually ensured the well-being of the much smaller workforce that remained.

came to California, expecting to settle in a sunny land of abundant fruits and good jobs, and who found instead hostility and hunger. Writing angrily to a friend, Steinbeck described the situation in the interior valleys:

There are about five thousand families starving to death over there, not just hungry but actually starving. The government is trying to feed them and get medical attention to them with the fascist groups of utilities and banks and huge growers sabotaging the thing all along the line and yelling for a balanced budget.

Then in 1937 Steinbeck and his wife motored along Route 66, the road taken by hundreds of thousands of migrants from the stricken farmlands of Oklahoma to California. This was the seed of *The Grapes of Wrath*, which chronicles the eviction of the Joads, an "Okie" farming family, and their journey to the promised land of California.

48 Rural poverty: tenant farmers in the cotton belt, photographed by Walker Evans for the book *Let Us Now Praise Famous Men*.

Cotton-growers were among the hardest hit of all farmers. "King Cotton" had enjoyed a long reign, and over the vast areas of the American South and South-West it was the only crop under cultivation. The disadvantages of this were that there was no alternative crop to sell when times were bad, and that the single-crop system exhausted the soil, turning it to dust. The typical farmer was a sharecropper – a tenant farmer who paid for his occupancy of the land, and often for his equipment and fertilizers, by giving the owner a large percentage of the crop he raised. Except during boom times (and there were no boom times once the First World War was over), the sharecropper lived well below the poverty line, eternally in and out of debt to his landlord. A classic book of reportage, *Let Us Now Praise Famous Men* (1939) by James Agee and Walker Evans, shows just how bad conditions were in the South; Agee's high-flown writing is not to all tastes, but Evans'

photographs constitute an instantly accessible account of rural poverty.

Pinched though their lives were, the tenant farmers clung stubbornly to their homes, even when Depression-hit "dust-bowl" states such as Oklahoma were struck by new calamities: the great storms of the mid-1930s, which swept away the crumbling, exhausted topsoil of their holdings. When families such as the Joads were evicted, they were bewildered. Surely the land was really theirs?

. . . it's our land. We measured it and broke it up. We were born on it, and we got killed on it, died on it. Even if it's no good, it's still ours. That's what makes it ours – being born on it, working on it, dying on it. That makes ownership, not a paper with numbers on it.

49 The "dustbowl": an abandoned Oklahoma farm, its soil ruined by wind erosion.

But they had to go, all the same. In *The Grapes of Wrath*, the Joads, like all the others, sell their familiar plough and tools and animals for anything they can get. Grampa Joad refuses to go, and has to be drugged with medication. But "Grampa an' the old place, they was jus' the same thing", and he dies soon afterwards, the first of several victims in the family's fight to survive.

The Grapes of Wrath gives a vivid account of the Joads' journey along Route 66 in an old truck. To them it is a new world whose values are so different that Pa is replaced as head of the family by Ma, who is determined to keep them together at all costs. Sharing hardships with other migrant families at temporary camp sites, and moved on by border guards, they reach California. But even before they cross the Mojave Desert into the lush heart of the state, they are warned about what to expect by a man and his son who are leaving – going back home, where things are no better but they can at least starve among friends. Wherever they come from, the man tells Ma's son, Tom Joad, they will be sneered at as "Okies":

Well, Okie use' ta mean you was from Oklahoma. Now it means you're a dirty son-of-a-bitch. Okie means you're scum.

Californians, clinging to their security, fear the Okies as invaders, desperate have-nots whose presence makes them feel threatened. Tom's informant tells him:

I hear there's three hundred thousan' of our people there – an' livin' like hogs, 'cause everything in California is owned. They ain't nothin' left. An' them people that owns it is gonna hang on to it if they got ta kill ever'body in the worl' to do it. An' they're scairt, an' that makes 'em mad.

The Joads soon discover the truth of this. The Okies are bullied and abused by the police, and harrassed and moved on except in places where they can be exploited as cheap labour, undercutting regular workers. The Joads lead a hand-to-mouth existence, occasionally earning a dollar or two and living in squalid "Hoovervilles" – shanty towns, derisively named after the ex-president. They enjoy only one civilized interlude, when they stop at a camp run by the federal government, where decent living conditions are provided and migrants are treated with the respect due to human beings. But there is little work nearby, and the Joads are forced to move into a new area. There they become involved in a strike and begin to understand the lesson of their experience: that, in the face of brutality and exploitation, their only hope lies in working with and caring for other men and women. The family is a fundamental value, and the human endurance embodied in Ma Joad is heroic in quality; but these are not enough. Ma's son, Tom Joad, follows in the footsteps of his visionary friend Casy, who has been murdered by strike-breaking thugs. Tom tells Ma, "I know now a fella aint no good alone." And he leaves the family to work among the strikers. At the end of the book, Tom's fractious, selfish sister, Rose of Sharon, who has just lost her baby, makes her own gesture of human solidarity, when she uses her milk-swollen breasts to suckle a wasted, dying stranger.

50 A still from the film of Steinbeck's novel *The Grapes of Wrath*. It shows the Joad family, on their way to the "promised land" of California, trying to get their overloaded Model T Ford back on the road.

GLOSSARY

American Dream Term often used to describe the prosperity and fulfilment that Americans expect from their way of life.

Authoritarian Applied to forms of government in which authority is emphasized at the expense of popular or individual rights. A useful term with which to describe ultra-right-wing or military parties or rulers that fall short of outright fascism (see below).

Capitalism Ideal or system in which most property, industries, businesses, etc. are privately owned, in contrast with socialism (see below).

Communist Supporter or member of a Communist Party, dedicated to the overthrow of capitalism (see above).

Dividend Payment made to a shareholder, representing his or her share of a company's profits.

Fascism The system of ideas and values associated with Nazi Germany, Fascist Italy and certain other states. Fascism is characterized by dictatorship, a cult of the leader, the militarization of society and the suppression by force of all opposition.

Five Year Plan Blueprint for economic development, regularly adopted since 1928 by the USSR, whose "planned economy" seemed an attractive alternative to the economic chaos in capitalist countries hit by the Depression.

GNP Gross National Product – a country's total output of goods and services.

Gold Standard Economic arrangement to stabilize the value of a currency by making it exchangeable for gold at a fixed rate. As a result of the disruption caused by the Depression, most countries abandoned the Gold Standard.

Indentures Agreement setting out the conditions governing an apprenticeship.

Industrial averages A series of average figures, calculated (in the New York *Times*) daily from the share prices of certain important industrial concerns. The rise or fall of these "industrials" was one way of assessing the state of the stock market.

Investor Person who puts up money to finance an industry or business, usually by buying shares in a company.

Laissez faire Doctrine that the state should not interfere in the operation of a country's economy.

Légion d'Honneur The Legion of Honour, a decoration awarded by the French government.

Means Test Government authorized investigation of household income, carried out to determine whether or not an unemployed person was entitled to the dole.

Monopoly Situation in which there is only one seller in a market. Absence of competition usually means that the monopoly can charge excessively high prices.

New Deal Name given to the policies adopted by the American President F.D. Roosevelt from 1933 to combat the Depression.

Pawn shop A place in which people are lent money on the security of goods which they leave with the pawnbroker. If the goods are not redeemed after a certain time, they are forfeited.

Popular Front Alliance of liberal, socialist, communist and other anti-fascist groups. During the 1930s there were Popular Front governments in France and Spain.

Protectionism Policy of protecting home industries by means of tariffs (see below).

Rationalization Policy of strengthening industries in difficulties by amalgamations and elimination of the weakest firms.

Relief American term for "the dole".

Socialism Ideal or system in which most industries, trading organizations, etc. are publicly owned.

Speculator Person who buys stocks and shares with an eye to quick profits rather than long-term investment.

Tariff A duty or tax levied on foreign goods coming into a country. This is often done to make them more expensive, so that they cannot compete with home-produced goods.

Third Reich Name of the regime established in Germany by Hitler and the Nazis.

Weimar Republic German republic (1919-33), overthrown by Nazis.

DATE LIST

1929 Labour government in Britain.
Herbert Hoover US President.
Share prices on Wall Street peak, then
collapse: the Crash.

1930 J.M. Keynes, *A Treatise on Money*.
Nazis' first great success in German
elections.

1931 Failure of Viennese Kreditanstalt: collapse of
Central and East European economies.
National Government in Britain: Gold
Standard abandoned; Means Test
introduced; Invergordon naval mutiny.
Japan occupies Manchuria.

1932 Suicide of Ivar Kreuger.
Depression at its height.

1933 Nazis take power in Germany.
Epidemic bank failures in USA; Roosevelt
becomes President, introduces New Deal;

USA abandons Gold Standard.

1934 Stavisky riots in France.

1935-6 Italian conquest of Ethiopia.

1936 Germans reoccupy Rhineland.
Outbreak of Spanish Civil War.
Jarrow March.
Keynes, *General Theory of Employment,
Interest and Money*.

1937 New recession in USA.
Japan wages war on China.

1938 Hitler incorporates Austria into Third Reich.
Munich crisis: large areas of
Czechoslovakia ceded to Germany.

1939 Fascists victorious in Spanish Civil War.
Britain and France at war with Nazi Germany.

1941 Germany attacks USSR.
Japan enters war, which becomes
world-wide.

BOOKS FOR FURTHER READING

Introduction
J.K. Galbraith, *The Great Crash*, Deutsch, 1954;
Penguin paperback, 1975
John Harris, *The Big Slump*, Zenith paperback,
1967
Isabel Leighton (ed.), *The Aspirin Age 1919-1941*,
Bodley Head, 1950; Penguin paperback, 1964
John Stevenson and Chris Cook, *The Slump*, Cape,
1977
Gordon Thomas and Max Morgan-Witts, *The Day
The Bubble Burst*, Hamish Hamilton, 1979;
Arrow paperback, 1980

Terkel
Studs Terkel, *Hard Times: An Oral History of the
Great Depression*, Allen Lane, 1970
Studs Terkel, *Talking to Myself*, Wildwood, 1977

Greenwood
Walter Greenwood, *Love on the Dole*, Cape, 1933;
Penguin paperback, 1942; many subsequent
editions

Kreuger
Helen Forrester, *Twopence to Cross the Mersey*,
Cape, 1974; Fontana paperback, 1981
Robert Shaplen, *Kreuger: Genius and Swindler*,
Deutsch, 1961

Wilkinson
Betty D. Vernon, *Ellen Wilkinson*, Croom Helm,
1982
Ellen Wilkinson, *The Town That Was Murdered*,
Gollancz, 1939

Hannington

Wal Hannington, *Never on Our Knees*, Lawrence and Wishart, 1967

Shirer

William L. Shirer, *The Rise and Fall of the Third Reich*, Secker, 1960; Pan paperback, 1964

William L. Shirer, *The Collapse of the Third Republic*, Heinemann, 1970; Pan paperback, 1972

William L. Shirer, *The Nightmare Years 1930-1940*, Little, Brown, 1984; Bantam paperback, 1985

Isherwood

Christopher Isherwood, *Mr Norris Changes Trains*, Hogarth Press, 1935; various paperback editions

Christopher Isherwood, *Goodbye to Berlin*, Hogarth Press, 1939; various paperback editions

Christopher Isherwood, *Christopher and His Kind 1929-1939*, Eyre Methuen, 1977

Keynes

D.E. Moggridge, *Keynes*, Fontana Modern Masters (paperback), 19

Joan Robinson, *Economic Philosophy*, Watts, 1962; Penguin paperback, 1964

Goebbels

"Joseph Goebbels" in Joachim C. Fest, *The Face of the Third Reich*, Weidenfeld, 1970; Penguin paperback, 1972

Roosevelt

Michael Rawcliffe, *The Roosevelt File*, Batsford, 1980

Capra

Richard Schickel, *The Men Who Made The Movies*, Hamish Hamilton, 1977

Brecht

Martin Esslin, *Brecht: A Choice of Evils*, Methuen, 4th edition, 1984

John Willett, *The Weimar Years*, Thames and Hudson, 1984

Shahn

James Thrall Soby, *Ben Shahn*, Penguin, 1947

Steinbeck

James Agee and Walker Evans, *Let Us Now Praise Famous Men*, 1939; first British edition published by Peter Owen, 1965

John Steinbeck, *In Dubious Battle*, Heinemann, 1936

John Steinbeck, *The Grapes of Wrath*, Heinemann, 1939; Penguin paperback, 1951

ACKNOWLEDGMENTS

The Author and Publishers would like to thank the following for permission to reproduce illustrations: BBC Hulton Picture Library for figures 1, 2, 3, 4, 5, 7, 9, 10, 11, 12, 17, 18, 22, 25, 27, 28, 29, 32, 34 and 38; Imperial War Museum for figure 44; Library of Congress for figure 6; Mansell Collection for figure 42; National Film Archive for figures 13, 14, 39, 40, 43 and 50; National Portrait Gallery for figure 26; Popperfoto for the frontispiece and figures 15, 16, 19, 20, 21, 23, 24, 41 and 47; *Punch* for figures 30 and 31; Smithsonian Institution for figures 45 and 46; US Department of Agriculture for figures 48 and 49; Wiener Library for figure 33. The pictures were researched by Patricia Mandel.

INDEX